Publish and Profit

A 5-STEP SYSTEM FOR ATTRACTING PAYING
COACHING AND CONSULTING CLIENTS,
TRAFFIC AND LEADS,
PRODUCT SALES
& SPEAKING ENGAGEMENTS

MIKE KOENIGS
Nine-Time #1 Bestselling Author

TABLE OF CONTENTS

ENDORSEMENTS

"There are those who lead and those who follow and then there are trend creators. Mike is the latter who uses his creative genius and relentless pursuit of new frontiers and technologies to change the landscape of what is possible and usable in today's crazy, ever-changing business landscape."

John Assaraf, NY Times Bestselling Author, Founder PraxisNow.com

"Mike Koenigs gives authors a clear blueprint on how to turn their ideas into books, self-publish those books through Amazon, and then market those books to readers online. Self-publishing a book can be scary. Self-publishing a book well can be a mystery. Publish & Profit demystifies the process for anyone who follows Mike's 5 simple steps."

Celeste Fine, Literary Agent, Sterling Lord Literistic

"I feel very blessed to have Mike Koenigs as a friend and in my personal and business life. After many years of teaching people around the world, it is guys like Mike Koenigs that keeps me sharp. And, we both share the same goals of wanting to help millions of entrepreneurs achieve their goals to greater financial and business success. More people need to engage in Mike's teachings – quite amazing!"

Brian Tracy, Author, Speaker, Entrepreneur

"There are very few visionaries who can truly look into the future and pluck from thin air the next big thing, not just once, but time after time - Tom Peters, Faith Popcorn, Sean Parker. Mike Koenigs breathes that rarified air. He's done it no less than eleven times over the past 20 years. But, unlike most, Mike not only sees the future, he monetizes it. In each of those eleven cases he took his vision and turned it into a successful million dollar plus business in fewer than 100 days. Whether he is teaching based on actual results (not theory), simplifying complex systems into digestible bites, extracting the genius from interviews with the most interesting people in the world or selling millions in front of the camera, I can think of no one better equipped to share with you the actionable knowledge Mike has distilled into his latest book."

Roland Frasier - CEO, All Channels Media

"Publish & Profit holds the key to creating a sustainable business that optimizes your income and your impact. The easy-to-implement, step-by-step process outlined by Mike in this book will help thousands of business owners create the positioning they need to gain the profits they seek. Mike is the real deal–take advantage of his wisdom, experience and know-how to help you focus on what really matters in your business and get results."

Pam Hendrickson, Bestselling Author, Product Creation Expert and co-founder of Make Market Launch IT

"Building a business or product takes a lot of work and is usually too daunting so most of us fail. But then there is Mike Koenigs. I have never seen anyone else have such a passion and ability to automate, teach and simplify any business process. He helps turn anyone into a superstar business stud. Thanks Mike!"

Eric Berman, CEO of Brandetize

"Mike Koenigs and I are in a mastermind group together and I have known him for several years. He is without question one of the smartest marketers I know. He's also one of the most deliberate, studied, systematic, focused and scientific entrepreneurs I know. I would recommend anything Mike produces because it is always top quality and delivers massive value. When it comes to business, he's the guy you want to be when you grow up :)"

Glen Ledwell CEO & Co Founder, Mind Movies LLC

"Mike never ceases to amaze me with his ability to spot and capitalize cutting edge business and marketing trends and then turn around and make it simple for anyone else to do the same. From the tools he creates to the training he provides, Mike knows what it takes to succeed quickly. As a bestselling publisher and consultant myself, I have often found myself asking "What would Mike Do?" Instead of reinventing the wheel, I simply steer it in his direction. Many people achieve success, only a few people can lead others to success as well as Mike Koenigs."

Brad Costanzo, CEO of Costanzo Marketing Group and Host of Bacon Wrapped Business

"4 Years ago I was ready for a huge transition in my business and my life. I sought out the advice of many "Gurus" for advice and found that many did not fulfill what they promised. When I stumbled on a video from Mike Koenigs, my heart began to sing and my mind began to whirl. This was the first time I had seen an expert who was heart-centered and serious about his big mission of helping mentor people into millionaire status. I purchased my first product from Mike and it seriously over-delivered. I applied the teachings to my business and was able to make $32,000 in one weekend! These past four years I have continued to be a fan of Mike and my business has grown exponentially. Mike is an amazing man on a serious mission to do good in this world, you'll love his work!"

Jessica Brace, Video Visibility Expert

"I found Mike Koenigs and his training and products 5 years ago. Who knew then that the things he teaches would completely change my life? I am now the author of 4 best-selling books, have a YouTube channel with almost 2,000,000 views, have been on The Today Show, and am changing my business model from one that required me to do everything, to one that does it all for me. Mike is the real deal, and the information in this book will help you go beyond your dreams too."

Sandi Masori, CBA "America's Top Balloon Expert"

"This book is one of very few books that outlines a system that actually works. I've used Mike's systems and strategies to position myself, expand my reach and rapidly multiply my business and income. Apply what Mike teaches in Publish and Profit and doors will open that you never thought possible. The strategies in this book are so brilliantly laid out that even a nine-year-old girl wrote four bestselling books in under 90 days. Mike Koenigs is a great friend, colleague and mentor to me but what sets him apart from others in the marketplace is he actually cares about his clients and wants us to succeed."

Jimmy Harding

"The day we were introduced to Mike Koenigs, his programs and his outstanding products our business marketing strategies radically changed. Our efforts became much more effective and enjoyable. With Mike's systems and passion for helping entrepreneurs like us succeed, we have transformed how we create, promote and deliver our own products and services. Now we are able to more easily reach the people that need us most. Also, we are both best-selling authors multiple times! Like Mike, helping our clients achieve their dreams make what we do every day worthwhile."

Dr. Thomas W. and Karol Clark, Center for Weight Loss Success, Newport News, VA

"It has been both a privilege and blessing to have come to know and learn from Mike Koenigs. I have directly benefitted from his personal and professional tutelage, as have countless individuals and entrepreneurs. By leveraging what Mike taught me I was able to establish a thriving consulting and app development business. Because of his care, products and teaching I was able to walk away from a career I no longer enjoyed and 'fired' my boss in the most Epic of ways. I was able to tell my boss I had some 'good news and some bad news'! My boss immediately knew I was resigning and asked what the 'Good News' was? In what seemed like slow motion and with a perfect delivery, I replied "I just saved $500 on my car insurance by switching to GEICO!" and walked out to a set of stunned, wide-open jaws of staff members and a shocked former boss! It is with pleasure and gratitude that I greatly recommend Mike Koenigs and his work."

Drew Griffin | App Developer | App Labs | Podcasting Magazine

"The first time I had the chance to see Mike Koenigs speak, I was hooked. What a peaceful, positive, and powerful presence. I learned so much about marketing and building my platform and was able to implement it into my business right away. He changed my perspective on content creation, video marketing, and has proven that service is the fastest road to success."

Ben Gioia, Speaker, Author, and Coach, Marketing With A Heart

"I joined one of Mike's programs, Instant Customer in the fall of 2011 and attended my first event in February of 2012. Right from the beginning, Mike treated me as though I had known him for 20 years. My challenge became to try and figure out how to best utilize the tools. The answer was to watch Mike and apply his same approach to my business. The strategy worked and has continued to work to this day. He talks about visualizing your favorite customer to achieve success, Mike has become my favorite inspiration."

Pat Ziemer

"With Mike's products you can become an expert immediately, the tools, courses and classes teach you basic to advanced techniques, the technology makes everything easy. To me this is the jump that I needed to take my business to the next level. I wrote my first two books in only three weeks in Spanish and English and they became instant bestsellers that got me booked on two radio shows that same week. Thank you Mike and everyone at Instant Customer!"

Georgina Salgado Sanchez, Wellness Consultant

"I've been working with Mike for over 5 years. Because of Mike, I have a profitable business and career. My kids and I are enjoying what life has to offer because I applied the skills and teachings he gave. Mike is full of golden nuggets and from the beginning I have used his expertise to boost my life and my business. Mike has been a mentor to me, honest, smart and on top of technology. A true giver who exceeds my expectations every time I see him. Mike is my friend and teacher. I am so grateful to have him on my team!"

Jenn Foster

"Mike Koenigs is one of the brightest entrepreneurs I know, he is a genius when it comes to developing software like Traffic Geyser. I first encountered him in 2010 when I was first captivated by video marketing. He and his entire crew have been a huge inspiration for me. Because of Publish and Profit, I wrote a book in literally a weekend, launched it and achieved #1 bestseller in 3 categories. I am looking forward to a long relationship with Mike Koenigs and Instant Customer. Publish And Profit has been the one tool that made me take action."

Garry I Wise, Pioneer Publishing

"Mike Koenigs has an uncanny ability to see where marketing and technology are headed and be there to meet them when the future arrives (probably grinning and asking "what kept you?"). There is no one better to watch if you want to stay ahead of the curve in marketing and business. If your livelihood depends on charging people for the "grey stuff" between your ears then this is a book you need to read and if you value your friends and colleagues, you should get them to read it too."

Rob Cuesta, 5-Time #1 Bestselling Author, CEO of HyperSuasion Consulting Ltd

"Mike Koenigs creates genius online marketing systems. His breadth of knowledge translates into easy, powerful actionable information that will get you the results you seek."

Lisa Thorp, CEO Thorp Institute and co-founder IntellBio Incs

"For a new writer like me who thought it was impossible, this book opened up the creative and marketing doors to publishing. It gave clear direction on everything from how to effortlessly create content to how best promote the book. This will help you create a book or books to help your cause or your business."

John G. Kelly, Founder of Find Local Customers Online

"Mike is the most forward-thinking, analytical, trend-spotting and first-to-market entrepreneur I know. There is a genius in him for business and profit creation. What I most admire and respect about Mike is he is real, down-to-earth and genuine on-stage and off-stage, always thinking about how he can create value for the good of many and help others bring out the genius in themselves. Because of Mike, I was able to clarify my business, publish my first book, and expand my business 10x just within a year's time. Mike has also given me a lot of courage and hope while I recover from cancer. This is a book that everyone should read If you want to learn from the best of the best and from the real-deal."

Irene Tomoe Cooper, International Love Coach

"Mike Koenigs is a rare individual and somewhat of an enigma. He is a true entrepreneur who has a great focus on seeing his clients reach success with his tools, products, teaching and information. Although he always seems to be going at 300 mph, his content and tools are solid and very, very effective and although he keeps himself very busy, he cares so much for his clients that he takes time and not least interest in securing their successes. I have studied under a long list of some of the world's greatest "gurus" among which Mike Koenigs truly is a star. He has rare authenticity and honesty. I have had the privilege to meet in person many, many of these satisfied clients. Mike and his tools and teachings are helping change the world for the better, empowering ordinary people to create wonderful lifestyles of their dreams and freedom that prior would have eluded them. A lot of Mike's tools are focused on automating processes and saving you huge amounts of time. I strongly recommend anyone to look into what Mike has to offer and not least to keep an eye on him for all future as he has an ability to connect the dots that most others don't see."

Mikkel Pitzner

"Mike is a visionary! Mike is able to predict and see trends in business, marketing and technology that are at least 12-18 months ahead of the time. Mike then translates those trends into practical, tactical and systemized tools and strategies for the everyday entrepreneur and business owner. Who else has more tangible documented proof that they have helped a high percentage of entrepreneurs and business owners? Who else has training, tools and systems that have helped hundreds of people become authors, with a great many being #1 best sellers. Who is better qualified to talk about "Publish and Profit" than a 9-Time #1 Best Selling Author who has written books to launch his businesses and built businesses around books? Nobody! This is a book that will help you "Share Your Knowledge, Become an Authority and Get Wealthy with a Purpose.""

John A. McCabe, 2 Time #1 Bestselling author, CEO & Founder, Real Estate Services

ACKNOWLEDGEMENTS

The original edition of this book was written, edited and published in only eight days. Well, eight days, 20 years of mistakes, and a team of dedicated team members and wonderful clients and customers who provided inspiration and success stories from the field. I'm so grateful for the support and patience you've given me.

Vivian Glyck and Zakary Koenigs, my incredibly patient wife, son and my family, Mom, Dad, my sister Ellen, and brothers Rick and Joel. I love you all so much. You are reminders the amazing gift life is.

Ed Rush, the most productive man in the world who became my marketing savior and voice when I didn't have one…You've consistently risen way above the call of duty and outperform like nobody I've ever known. I'd take a bullet for you, brother.

Gene Naftulyev my friend of 30 years who helped restore my business health when my health failed. I can't tell you how much I value what you've done for family, my business and me this when I was being treated for cancer and beyond.

Chris and Pam Hendrickson, best of friends and my family here in San Diego.

Arielle Ford and Brian Hilliard, your unconditional love and support keeps me connected to the divine when I lose my way.

JJ Virgin my "sista from another mista" – soul sister, the most generous and abundance-minded person I know. Your spirit, strength, power, conviction and brilliance is awe-inspiring and infectious.

Debbie Ford. RIP. I miss you, your spirit, sarcasm, cancer guidance, friendship and commitment to truth. Thank you for showing me my shadow even when I didn't want to see it.

Jessie Schwartzburg, you're an entrepreneur's dream and you make us (and me) look good with every event you touch. I hope we continue working together until we decide to quit working.

Joe Polish - thank you for your kindness and support over the past ten years. Thank you for the continued introductions and connections.

Tony Robbins, Dean Graziosi, Bill Glazer, Dan Kennedy for your guidance, brilliance and inspiration you've given me over the years.

Lee Stein, Dan Sullivan and Jim Kennedy - my great mentors. I look up to you. I want to be like you someday.

My San Diego mastermind brothers: Ed Rush, John Assaraf, Darren Hardy, Eric Berman, Greg Habstritt, Bob Serling, Steven Cox, Matt Trainer. You guys are an inspiration and motivating force that helped keep me alive when I almost died from cancer.

And to my newest San Diego mastermind "gang": Mike Filsaime, Eric Berman, Nick Unsworth, Brad Costanzo, Glen Ledwell, Roland Frasier, Mark Anthony Bates, David Metzler, Jeff Smith, Larry Ostrovsky and Micha Mikailian. You're all rock stars. I love smart people and it's an honor to break bread and witness your genius and wisdom.

To my incredibly supportive JV partners and affiliates over the years. Without you, I wouldn't have a business. Thank you so much for believing and trusting in me.

To my JV partners, affiliates and friends in the marketing business: Alex Mandossian, Amish Shah, Amy Porterfield, Andy Jenkins, Bill and Steve Harrison, Brandon Lasaro, Brendon Burchard, Camper Bull, Casey Zeman, Cathy Demers, Chalene Johnson, Chris and Janet Attwood, Chris Burfield, Christian Mikelson, Damien Zamora, Dan O'Day, Daniel Hall,

Danny Eien, Darius M. Barazandeh, Dave Gambrill, Diego Rodriguez, Don Crowther, Ed Dale, Frank Kern, Jame Wedmore, Jay Niblick, Jeanne Hurlbert, Jeff Mills, Jeff Walker, Jernej Kriznar, Jimmy Harding, Lisa Sasevich, John Assaraf, John Barry, John Kremer, Jon Benson, Jon Walker, Jules Watkins, Justin Livingston, Kalem Aquil, Kenny Reuter and Travis from Kajabi, Kevin Harris, Kris Gilbertson, Marissa Murgatroid, Mark Harris, Mary Ellen Tribby, Miguel De Jesus, Mike Filsaime, Mike LeMoine, Milana Leshinsky, Rich Cook, Rich German, Robert Evans, Robert Hughes, Sean Malarky, Shelley Hitz, Shinichi Sasaki, Stephen Renton, Steve Olscher, Steve Sipress, Susan Harrow, Teofilo Bajar, Tiffany Kennedy, Todd Gross, Wendy Stevens and Yanik Silver.

My wonderful customers and clients. You're my inspiration and mission! It's an honor and a privilege to serve and support you.

I want to give a big SHOUT OUT to my "experimental" customers who participated in the creation of the Publish and Profit training system. 78% of you wrote, published, promoted and became #1-#3 bestselling authors in less than three weeks! Congratulations! This system works and it's been a dream come true to watch you succeed, thrive and change lives!

Here you are, in no particular order: Ben Pritchett, Carlos Barroso, Carlos Marin, Charles Rankin, Diane Bell, Frank Velazquez, Gary Rush, Grahame Rees, Jim Butz, Ben Pritchett, Carlos Barroso, Carlos Marin, Charles Rankin, Diane Bell, Frank Velazquez, Gary Rush, Grahame Rees, Joe Quartana, Karol Clark, Miguel de Jesus, Steven Laurvick, Niki Faldemolaei, Steven Laurvick, Tracy Ross, Ben Farmer, Siou F. Lee, Ian Bosler, Barry Gumaer, Dr. Lyndon Jones, Emma Thompson, Garry Wise, John Kelly, Joseph Spada, Sherah Thompson, Tom Woods, David Pittman, Georgina Salgado Chavez, John McCabe, Melanie Foster, Winifred Anderson, Rob Cuesta, Dale Bell, Judy Carrico, James Chandler, Thomas Watts, Bree Whitlock, Andy Broadaway, John Cote, Jennifer Cote, Everett O'Keefe, Sandi Masori, Leo Melendez, Carrie Smith, Rob Falco, Mark MacDonald, Tim Ringgold, Travis Houston and Camper Bull.

And everyone else I may have forgotten to give thanks and praise to. I love supporting and serving you. You are my big why and it's a deep and profound pleasure to watch your personal and business transformation.

Thank you for making this another bestseller - the 10th one in less than three years!

The first edition of this book was written, edited and published in only eight days. *Well, eight days, 20 years of mistakes, and a team of dedicated team members and wonderful clients and customers.* I'm so grateful for the support and patience you've given me.

Publish And Profit: A 5-Step System For Attracting Paying Coaching And Consulting Clients, Traffic And Leads,... by Mike Koenigs and Ed Rush (Oct 2, 2014)

$0.99 Kindle Edition
Auto-delivered wirelessly

★★★★★ ▾ (10)

#1 Best Seller in Business Leadership Training
Books: See all items

Product Details

File Size: 2999 KB

Print Length: 242 pages

Simultaneous Device Usage: Unlimited

Publisher: MikeKoenigs.com (October 2, 2014)

Sold by: Amazon Digital Services, Inc.

Language: English

ASIN: B00O4SCMW8

Text-to-Speech: Enabled ☑

X-Ray: Not Enabled ☑

Lending: Not Enabled

Amazon Best Sellers Rank: #698 Paid in Kindle Store (See Top 100 Paid in Kindle Store)
 #1 in Kindle Store > Kindle eBooks > Business & Money > Marketing & Sales > **Marketing**
 #1 in Books > Business & Money > Management & Leadership > **Training**
 #1 in Kindle Store > Kindle eBooks > Business & Money > Management & Leadership > **Training**

Mike Koenigs,
San Diego, California

FOREWORD

by F18 Fighter Pilot, USMC Ret., Ed Rush

To say that I am a big fan of checklists is an understatement.

If there was something called "Checklists Day" you can bet that I would be out on the curb, family in tow, wearing my "Happy Checklist Day" hat and blowing on a plastic kazoo during the annual Checklist Parade.

If there was a faith-based organization called the Checklistians, I'd join. And I would encourage everyone I knew to accept Checklists into their heart and donate to the cause.

If there was a Checklist Club that met the local park every Wednesday afternoon, I'd be there, bent over a Checklist Board, jumping my Checklists over my opponent's Checklists.

The reason why I love checklists is simple.

A checklist saved my life.

It was the day I found myself in a completely out-of-control F-18 fighter jet.

You see, I trained for years to master the weapons, tactics, and maneuvers in this $40 million dollar airplane. I executed training missions with the best and I deployed to far off places to meet the enemy.

But not *this* day.

This day I wasn't flying.

I was falling.

So what do you do when you've gotten your airplane in *that* spot?

What do you do when your fighter jet no longer responds to your commands?

What do you do when you have 27 seconds to live?

The answer is simple: **you follow the checklist.**

The F-18 Out of Control Procedure goes like this:

1. Controls - RELEASE, FEET OFF RUDDERS, SPEEDBRAKE IN
   If still out of control...
2. Throttles - IDLE
3. Altitude, AOA, airspeed and yaw rate - CHECK
4. When recovery indicated by AOA and YAW rate tones removed, side forces subsided, and airspeed accelerating above 180 KCAS -
5. Recover

That day I executed my checklist perfectly.

And I am here to tell you the story of an almost-dead fighter pilot whose life was saved by following a proven formula.

And it's the same thing I love about Mike Koenigs' Publish and Profit program.

In its essence, Publish and Profit is a proven system that delivers everything it promises (and more). It contains the system, formula, procedures, and checklists to become a #1 best selling author every time.

I have personally used the principles behind Publish and Profit to create and launch four #1 best selling books in less than 3 years...and I used the "how to make money from your book" principles to build high 6-figure businesses that I grew and sold.

To put it simply: this system works.

But only when you work the system.

This book can serve as a wonderful coaster to put under a water glass. It will look nice on your bookshelf. And it can help you start a blazing beach bonfire.

But If I may offer a small suggestion, this book works best when you roll up your sleeves and read it with an eye for...

IMPLEMENTATION.
(my favorite word BTW)

Imagine it's just 6 months from now. You've published your book. You've hit the bestseller lists. Radio and TV producers are calling you out of the blue. New leads, customers, and clients are coming into your business. You've paid off your debts. You're experiencing the joy of passive income. And you can finally afford that vacation of a lifetime.

It all happened because of your book.

Actually, it all happened because you decided to get rid of all the excuses and finally share your message with the world.

This is where you begin.

INTRODUCTION

Dear Friend,

Welcome to Publish and Profit.

This represents nearly 20 years of hard work, experience and the efforts of my incredible team and customers. Maybe you're one of them!

I wanted to take a moment to share some thoughts with you in no particular order about what to expect in this book.

First, it's interactive. There are lots of opportunities for you to go deeper in the content, gain access to free training videos, participate in some interactive webcast events and more.

Second, this book is for business. It's intended to help you grow your business, produce qualified leads and make money. It isn't intended to serve poets, fiction-writers or people who want to write memoirs, children's books or novels.

Third, it's for implementers. You'll see there's LOTS of ideas that you can use to grow any business type. If you're the type who's looking for free, easy money, this isn't the book for you. I'm not here to blow smoke up your butt and lie to you.

Fourth, this book wasn't intended to be a NY Times #1 Bestseller. It's designed to start a conversation with you, give us a chance to get to know each other better, develop trust, a bond and ultimately help us decide if we will work together someday.

Fifth, this is a book that's packed with content and lots of ideas. It's a WHAT book, not a step-by-step HOW TO book. My intention and the purpose of this book is to show you the most powerful ways to market yourself, expose you to multiple ways to promote yourself with books, build a list, gain exposure and leverage the latest technology and strategies available and set yourself up for long-term growth and maybe a potential publishing deal in the future. We have a how-to system available that includes everything you need to execute what you read in these pages.

I'll be the first to admit, I'm a shameless self-promoter - and I want to help you reach more people, make more money and add value to your life and everyone you come in contact with. You'll notice there are opportunities throughout this book to register and watch videos and YES, I do have some great products I'd like to sell to you because they work and you'll have a better life with them.

Having said that, if you like what you read, or most of what you read, I'd absolutely, positively love to hear from you and get to know you better and find out what you learned - or better yet, post a picture or video on my facebook wall at <u>www.Facebook.com/YouEveryWhereNow</u> or Tweet me at @YouEverywhere.

The BEST way to start a relationship with me will be to visit the web link below, watch the free training webinars, and learn more about how to grow your business and brand.

I'm looking forward to getting to know you better!

Sincerely,

Mike Koenigs in San Diego, California, USA

FREE BOOK UPDATES AND VIDEO TRAINING

This book is INTERACTIVE - to get free training videos, a free audiobook and updates to this book:

visit www.PublishAndProfit.com/BookBonus
or text your email address to (858) 707-7417

CHAPTER ONE

The Most Powerful Marketing Tool In The World

"Every great dream begins with a dreamer. Always remember, you have within you the strength, the patience, and the passion to reach for the stars to change the world."

Harriet Tubman

Dear friend,

I want to share with you the single most powerful tool to promote and market your business, give you celebrity status, attract better customers, multiply your income, become recession and competition-proof and give you more freedom, autonomy and happiness.

And I'll show you irrefutable proof that this works in any business or industry, online and offline, in any language, anywhere in the world.

This solution is 564 years old.

It's not high-tech.

It's built armies and won wars, as well as the hearts and minds of entire countries.

It's endured the test of time.

And it can create wealth and fame for those who understand it's potential...

With it, you suddenly have crowds surrounding you, shouting "You! You! You!" *instead of you screaming after them*, "Me! Me! Me!"

It's like getting an exclusive VIP ticket to a private members-only club, filled with a community that enables your freedom and autonomy... and you're going to learn the "secret knock" that will get you past the "velvet rope".

What is it, you ask?

What is this magical secret thing that can bring you fame, fortune and wealth?

It's a book.

It's *your* book.

You see, you can wrap a book around your business... or you can wrap a business around your book. But really, it's not about the book, it's about the power a book will give you; and with it, you can access almost the entire human race, can connect with an audience, share your message, sell more products, create buzz, and have real authority and credibility in any market.

You're about to learn a completely new model for either starting or enhancing any business - an "Integrated Hybrid Publishing System" that is being embraced by small business owners, NY literary agents, *NY Times* bestselling authors, experts, speakers, consultants, coaches, CEOs and entrepreneurs - many of whom are hearing about it for the first time.

You may think you've heard this before or maybe you have even already published a book; but my guess is you also may not have the freedom and authority you wanted when you first began. It's okay… and it's not your fault.

What you're about to experience is a *new way to think*, so hang on. You're about to discover a completely different way to leverage your book… and you're also about to see how quickly you can achieve the income and results you want.

With it, you'll meet dozens of people from all walks of life; from Fortune 5 executives to balloon artists who are growing their influence, authority and income in these pages and you'll have a chance to watch several bonus videos that will walk you through the process too.

In this chapter, you'll learn the three fatal misconceptions you've been led to believe about being a successful author; and, even juicier, I'll show you a simple five-step system that you or anyone can use to overcome these challenges.

Please don't confuse my excitement with hype—I'm just so excited for you to be holding this book and learning these strategies. My goal for you is to show you a system and a business model that, up until now, only a few people know about... and it works like crazy.

So, who am I and why should you listen to me? If you don't know my story, I'm NOT a #1 *New York Times* bestselling author. In fact, I'm a product of 30 years of continuous rapid failures. I grew up in a lower-middle class family in the tiny town of 763 people in Eagle Lake, Minnesota. My dad's a barber. At 78, he still cuts hair. I didn't do well in a traditional classroom environment and got C to D grades...and I never went to college. It took me well into my 30s to discover I have five great skills and I'm horrible at another 5,000.

But you and I probably have some things in common: we both like to help people and we're fiercely independent; we're creative; we want our freedom and want to get ahead, right? We want to get paid what we're actually worth, not what we can get.

My story begins with me nearly losing everything...

Less than three years ago as of the time I'm writing this, I was separated 2,521 miles away from my family being treated for Stage 3a cancer at the Duke University Medical Center in North Carolina. I was surrounded by people who were dying while I fought for my life. That's when I became obsessed with the idea of writing a book in case I died, leaving my wife and my 10-year-old son, Zak, behind.

With only an hour of strength a day, waking up in a pile of my own hair that had fallen out of my head that night and armed only with my iPhone I wrote, published, promoted and became a #1 bestselling author in less than 30 days. Since then, using that same system, my team and I have helped over 500 people from age 5 to 80 write, publish, promote and become bestselling authors.

One of my favorite success stories is 9-year-old Abbey Richter, who wrote four bestselling books in only three months about rescue pets. She was featured in *American Girl* magazine and has been asked to speak at events and sign autographs. Her parents are veterinarians. Another is Andy Falco, a former K9 cop who left service after being injured on the job. He came to us on the verge of bankruptcy and foreclosure. He recently closed a $349,000 deal with the country of Bahrain… all because of a book!

And then there's [Joni], an 80-year old woman who went through bankruptcy, feeling lost and without hope, transform her life by writing four books in just three years, starting a consulting business

The great news is, I'm not dead. It's really nice to be alive. My doctors say I beat cancer, which means I can continue on my personal life mission of creating 1,000,000 entrepreneurs—and hopefully, 1,000,000 millionaires over the rest of my career!

I've also gone on to publish nine #1 bestselling books; and the "Publish and Profit" system continues to get better every day in our "living laboratory" of customers and clients in over 60 countries from every profession, languages and cultures.

Imagine this: could you become the next bestselling author like founder and publisher of the *Huffington Post*, Arianna Huffington, superstar author of *The 4-Hour Workweek* Tim Ferriss, or Jack Canfield, whose *Chicken Soup* series of books have sold over *half a billion copies?*

According to an article published in the *New York Times*, 81% of the United States population wants to write a book someday, or think they have a book inside them. Don't you? According to a recent article in *Forbes* magazine, 600,000 to 1,000,000 books are published every year in the United States alone. Most of them sell fewer than 250 copies in total, while others go on to sell millions. Why?

After working with so many people, we've found that most failed authors make three fatal mistakes which prevent them from either starting or finishing their book. And for the ones that do actually finish, here are the reasons why they aren't successful at marketing, promotion, sales or getting results.

The first mistake is the "Ernest Hemingway Excuse." That's thinking you have to be a writer in order to be an author. Nothing could be further from the truth. Look at nine-year-old Abbey Richter as an example—she's only nine and she wrote four books in just three months. I "wrote" my first book by talking into my iPhone.

Mistake number two is something we call the "Albert Einstein Assumption." That's thinking you actually have to be an expert or even smart in order to be an author of a book. I barely graduated high school and never went to college. Many of our clients and customers who are successful, profitable authors didn't start out feeling confident or prepared either. But they took a chance… and took action using a proven system… and now, their books are giving them the influence, income, authority, community and autonomy they deserve.

Don't you want the same thing?

Mistake number three is conveniently named after the third wealthiest person in the world. It's called "Warren Buffett BS." That's believing and thinking that you have to be rich or famous in order to be a successful published author.

It's just not true —none of our published students began with a silver spoon in their mouth. Neither did I. But they did have a system—a proven, tested, and refined five-step formula that will allow you to write, publish and profit from your books, even if you're not a writer.

And even though you don't have to start out being famous, a book is one of the very best ways to become famous… especially on your topic.

The Publish and Profit 5 Step System

---

*"Twenty years from now you will be
more disappointed by the things that you didn't do
than by the ones you did do."*

Mark Twain

Here is the system, the five steps to publishing and profiting from your book. These will work for you whether you're starting from scratch or even if you've already written a book and want to re-launch it.

STEP #1: PREPARE

This is the place to start… and sadly, this is where most aspiring authors get stuck… forever. We've simplified, streamlined and templatized the preparation process to help you get to the book faster and easily determine:

- What to write about
- Who to write your book for
- What to name your book - including how to create a great title and subtitle
- Your "hook" and story
- Your "package" the cover of your book

And if you're overwhelmed, don't know where to start, or even what to write about, don't worry. In the next chapter, we'll do an exercise together to guide you through the process and help you name your book and make a great book cover.

But for now, as Stephen Covey said, "Begin with the end in mind."

There are 10 primary reasons to write a book. Some of the most powerful are to make money, sell a product, grow your following or tribe, build your list, help a client or you have a message to share. Most people we have worked with have a dual motivation: they want to make money *and* share their message.

And in a later chapter, I'll show you the 11 ways to make money with your book.

STEP #2: PERFORM

Perform your content. You can do this in any number of simple ways: answering questions, telling stories or interviewing another expert. The great news is you can use this same step-by-step formula for creating videos, audios, books and products using this same system. It's not just for books!

Of course, you can type it all up using your computer. But that's tediously slow and often creates writer's block.

You don't need to lock yourself in a room or a cabin for three months of isolation, either.

The majority of clients who use our system create most of their book content in about four hours. That's a standard 140-page-book, which is the perfect length and an easy read.

In a recent training event, one of our customers, Georgina Salgado, performed her book and completed 23 chapters in a single evening! Three weeks later it was a bestseller and she was booked on the radio for multiple shows!

Healthy, Happy, Thin & Diet Free.: Discover the lies and little secrets from fitness industry, the weight loss... by Georgina Chavez (Sep 19, 2014)

$0.00 kindleunlimited
Subscribers read for less. Learn more.
$0.99 Kindle Purchase ✓Prime

Best Seller in Holistic Medicine
Kindle Store: See all items.

Happy Hormones, Slim Belly: Over 40? Lose 7 lbs. the First Week, and Then 2 lbs. Weekly-Guaranteed by Jorge Cruise (Dec 23, 2013)

$11.99 Kindle Edition
Auto-delivered wirelessly
$24.95 $19.38 Hardcover ✓Prime
Get it by Tuesday, Sep 23

★★★★☆ (183)
Other Formats: Paperback
Excerpt
Page 13 ...were a significant part of a healthy diet, but this conventional wisdom... See a random page in this book.

Here's a secret: your book doesn't have to be PERFECT. You can always update it later. It doesn't have to be your magnum opus. It's about ONE THING. It's about getting it DONE, so that you can connect with your ideal audience, grow your business and attract the right clients.

As long as you can answer questions, are passionate about what you're teaching or doing and like helping people, writing a book is purely a matter of following a system.

Here's the BIG SECRET: getting years of experience, your personal genius, your journey and your stories of how you've helped people throughout your career captured on paper is EASY once you've completed STEP #1!

STEP #3: PUBLISH

Your goal is to be seen, heard and read anywhere, everywhere, on any device and at any time. The biggest brands in the world including Google, Apple and Amazon will publish and pay you 70% for your content while promoting and marketing you to the world… and making sure you can be seen, heard and read on any internet-connected device.

PUBLISH means much more than ebooks and books.

Your book can be easily turned into podcasts, audiobooks, courses, products, events and training materials too.

Where is your content going to be consumed? Right now, there are:

- Almost 3 billion mobile smartphones in use worldwide
- About 3 billion internet-connected desktop and laptop computers
- Approximately 2 billion internet-connected tablets - iPads, Android, Kindle devices - and they are outselling computers
- Hundreds of millions of people drive their cars back and forth from work every day, and according to Neilson, 46% of them are listening to streaming audio or podcasts
- And then there are almost 300 million internet-connected televisions, Smart TVs and Apple TVs

Why is this so important to you?

Companies like Google, Amazon and Apple are in the ATTENTION BUSINESS, not the publishing business. Let me repeat that because this ONE DISTINCTION alone can completely change the way you think about what business you're in.

THEY, and YOU, are in the ATTENTION BUSINESS.

Google, Amazon and Apple sell mobile phones. They sell music, movies, television shows, books and magazines. They're all in the CREDIT CARD business… They are in your pocket, your bedroom, bathroom, living room, kitchen, on every screen, in your computer, television, car, schools, churches…and in your business.

They have UNLIMITED shelf space and unlimited access to you and your prospects. They're in virtually every country in the world, in practically every language.

And they've completely changed HUMAN BEHAVIOR over the past few years with IMPULSE BUYS. They sell us digital products for $0.99— useful apps, music, ebooks and books.

Heck, I know people who have purchased books, apps, music and movies while they're in the bathroom. I don't know about you, but these days the phone or tablet is everywhere within arm's reach!

THINK ABOUT IT. This is a GUARANTEED, PROVEN MODEL that is sitting on top of billions of dollars of infrastructure—and you have access to all of it... for FREE!

And right now, YOU can leverage this perfect storm:

- Your book becomes a one-click buy...
- It starts a conversation with a prospect...
- It encourages a relationship...with you on stage
- That builds trust...
- Suddenly, you're in every pocket, on every screen, being seen, heard, read, viewed, listened to, understood and adored by a growing audience all over the world...
- And with that relationship, you can sell your products, services or get paid just recommending other people's products...
- And the technology follows your prospects and customers everywhere! Even into the bathroom!

When you combine unlimited free distribution with unlimited free shelf space, and when you learn the "secret knock" strategy that we'll teach you in the next chapter, you'll learn how to attract, inspire, motivate and persuade an audience to want to do business with you!

THAT'S STEP #3: *PUBLISH*.

STEP #4: PROMOTE

The first and most obvious place is to promote your book to the important social media sites... for FREE. That's why I personally buy and promote every single one of my customer's books on my social media pages. It works!

A recent study by Pew Research reports that 73% of the human race actually engages with social media every month. That's 5.1 Billion people at your fingertips. Take a look at this—my wife and I do humanitarian work in Uganda. Five years ago, only the tribal leaders and chiefs had a simple Nokia phone that someone walked or biked to charge every few days. Now there are kids walking to school with Smartphones who want to follow me on Facebook! All that in five years!

By leveraging the free social distribution channels from Google, YouTube, Apple, Amazon, Facebook, Twitter, LinkedIn and dozens of other social sites, nearly the entire world can watch, listen or read your content.

Your book or audiobook becomes a conversation that you can use to educate and inspire your readers; to build a relationship on your terms with your language. And you can release it in as many formats and languages as you can imagine so it can be seen, heard, read or watched on any device, anywhere, anytime.

Your book provides a creative roadmap that can be easily turned into social media content, videos, articles, media hooks for television and radio, speeches and podcasts. How great does it feel when you have a map and system prepared for you, giving you guidance to whatever marketing or business destination you have planned for yourself?

Put your "imagination hat on" for just a few minutes and experience this as if the following has already happened…

Imagine:

- You've **PREPARED** your book using a simple system to grab your story, hook and message.
- You've **PERFORMED** by rapidly creating your book content by telling stories, answering questions or interviewing experts.
- You've **PUBLISHED** your content with the help of the biggest ATTENTION-GETTING brands in the world like Amazon, Apple, Google and more —so that your book can get everywhere with a 100% proven business model.

- You've **PROMOTED** your books on every major social site in the world, reaching 73% of the human race with a system that leverages the free audiences of the biggest brands in the world. 73%— that's 5.1 billion people!

You're a published author and people are coming to you. You're getting booked on radio, TV, podcast shows, speaking, presenting and changing lives...

They know and recognize you… and you have the credibility, gravitas and status to back it up.

Now it's time to leverage and monetize everything you've done into a business that pays you month in and month out; to create passive income streams that can give you the autonomy you want and the following you deserve.

STEP #5: PROFIT

Step number five is to profit from the exposure that your book gives you. Although getting monthly royalty checks are nice, that's not how you make money with books.

A book can get your foot in the door, bypass gatekeepers (you know those people who don't let you speak to the real decision-makers), get someone to take your call, get you on stage, in the media, etc. The list is endless.

But taken further, a book is a starting point: a framework. You can use a book to test out an idea to see if it captures and accesses an audience by leveraging the free publishing and promotion tools we'll cover in another chapter. What's more, the biggest publishers who realize they are in the ATTENTION business are there to MARKET YOU and PAY YOU for your content.

Your book is the WHAT, driving people to the HOW (those are your products, services, events, training programs, coaching, consulting or your solutions).

You're leveraging proven models. A $0.99 buyer IS A BUYER and when you use our proven influence and persuasion techniques to bring the reader, reader or listener to your business, they quickly and easily become a customer of your more expensive products and can even turn into a high-paying consulting client.

Once your book gains momentum, you can build a business around it and profit from that exposure. You can turn your books into products and services. It can be licensed. We've identified 10 different ways your book can generate profit for you! Or if you already have products and services, your book gives you more exposure, authority and celebrity so you become competition and recession-proof.

You can use your book to:

1. Create community and connection with your audience
2. Engage on social media
3. Build your list
4. Get booked for speaking and events
5. Promote live events
6. Use as a giveaway at trade shows
7. Fuel book and product launches
8. Promote during teleseminars, webinars and webcasts
9. Get consulting deals
10. Book royalties and publishing advances

This is only a beginning - the list is virtually endless and limited only by your imagination.

That's why we say you can wrap a business around your book or wrap a book around your business.

So how do you crack the code to build and create a successful publishing platform?

That's what **Publish and Profit** is all about. And if it hasn't become obvious already, this isn't just about books. This is much, much bigger than that.

Books are fame, authority and wealth multipliers.

It's a simple fact that published authors make more money, get more attention, have more freedom and are given more opportunities to share their important message with the world when they use a proven system to properly leverage books as multipliers. When you're an author, you're immediately perceived as a thought leader.

Books push you to the *front of the line*, bypass crowds, give you VIP access, walk the red carpet, get past velvet ropes, give you attention and the spotlight.... you get the best seats and tickets; recognition; fame; bigger paychecks and meetings with CEO and VIPs.

Ask anyone who has successfully written, published and promoted a book using a proven system about what their book has done for them...

Tony Robbins' books *Unlimited Power* and *Awaken the Giant Within* made him a worldwide sensation that gave him massive exposure and resulted in changing the lives of millions of people worldwide, including my own. His most recent book, "MONEY Master the Game: 7 Simple Steps to Financial Freedom" became an immediate bestseller and instantly positioned Tony as a financial and money guru because he interviewed nearly 50 of the most successful money gurus in the world.

Tim Ferriss coined the phrase lifestyle design; his books, *The 4-Hour Workweek, The 4-Hour Body* and *The 4-Hour Chef* made him an international superstar and established him as an angel investor in Twitter, Facebook, Uber and Evernote.

One of our customers, Karol Clark, grew a brick and mortar medical practice from the ground up, wrote three books in six months that have added over $140,000 in annual revenues and started a new consulting practice.

JJ Virgin, author of *The Virgin Diet* and several cookbooks and one of our customers, earns millions of dollars every year selling her nutritional shakes and bars, supplements, speaking and coaching programs... because of her books!

Just look at who's on TV, watch TED videos, and see who appears on the radio. Almost all of them are BESTSELLING AUTHORS!

Most of them didn't feel confident or clear when they started. Most didn't feel like their books were "done." But then their skepticism turned into amazement when the momentum and the opportunities opened up.

It's easier than ever to become a bestseller because all the biggest ATTENTION-GETTING tools and brands have conspired to make it possible to be everywhere, on every device instantaneously... and with the new Integrated Publish and Profit Hybrid Publishing Model, you're going to jump to the head of the line...

In the past, it took YEARS for successful authors to get to where they are because they didn't have a proven system to model.

By now, you may be thinking, "Great, that worked for them... but it won't work for my business." That's the second "big myth" objection I get from people who think a book won't work for them and their business.

Let me give you an example of one of our clients, Sandi Masori, who is a balloon artist. She used our system, wrote a book in less than 30 days, became a bestseller a few days later and ended up on *The Today Show*. Did I mention she's a *balloon artist*?

It also worked for former Marine Corps officer, John Cote, who used his book *Mobilize Your Customers* to become a niche authority in the medical tourism industry and to launch a podcast that is getting 100,000 downloads a month. John now speaks in front of thousands at industry events and has sponsors and advertisers competing against each other to advertise on his show. And the best part of the story? He didn't know anything about his niche a year ago.

Sandi and John didn't fall prey to the myth that their business was different... and you shouldn't either.

YOU ARE IN THE ATTENTION BUSINESS. Without it, your business is destined for failure because now there's more noise and more competition than ever, *everywhere*.

This dream has come true for me and my clients (including over 500 people who have used the system to write, publish and promote their first book) — kids as young as nine years old and another who's 79!

This system works in any country, in any language, for any business, without exception—and it will work for you and your business too.

In an upcoming chapter, you'll discover a simple formula to come up with the perfect book title in five minutes or less!

And in the last chapter is this book, you'll see brand-new breakthrough technology that will automate publishing, promotion, marketing and monetizing your book.

It's your time to shine. It's your time to be a star and it's your time to experience one of the greatest gifts you will ever receive: the smiling face of someone who walks up to you and says, "Thank you. Your book changed my life."

Welcome to more freedom and more income. Welcome to **Publish and Profit.**

CHAPTER THREE

Success Psychology and Mindset

"Take up one idea. Make that one idea your life—think of it, dream of it, live on that idea. Let the brain, muscles, nerves, every part of your body, be full of that idea, and just leave every other idea alone. This is the way to success."

Swami Vivekananda

Less than a month before I wrote the original edition of this book, we created "Publish and Profit," a step-by-step training course about how to publish, promote, and become a best-selling author. We had 39 customers who paid us thousands of dollars to attend a live workshop to learn this process, and we guided them through everything they need to know to prepare, perform, publish, promote, and profit from their book ideas.

Within three days, everyone who attended clearly understood "why" they wanted to write a book, the benefits a book would provide for their business, what their content was going to be, a high quality title and subtitle for their book. We had designers in the room that made book covers for their book. We helped everyone establish a clear vision of the content of their book. Within three weeks of completing the course, 26 of those 39 people had become best-selling authors and within 8 weeks almost all of them were published and profitable. Most of them wouldn't consider themselves to be writers in the first place.

A few of the most interesting examples include Andy Broadaway who not only published one book, but 2 books (both at #1 Best Seller). He also helped his 17-year-old son write and publish his first book (#3). HIs 4th book involved a client and #1 bestseller status, all in 30 days. Another example is Sandi Masori. Sandi came up with an idea for her fourth book, and within seven days, the *DIY Balloon Bible For All Seasons: How to Wow Your Friends and Impress Your Relatives With Amazing, Easy Balloon Decorations* became a #1 bestseller in three different categories and reached an Amazon bestseller rank of #1,584— which is pretty high for a book that sells for $2.99.

Other examples include John Cote who converted 16 episodes of his *Healthcare Elsewhere* podcast into a book with which he began promoting his services to an audience he knew nothing about one year ago, and several first-time authors, including Jim Butz, Carrie Smith, Garry Wise, John McCabe, and several others also published and promoted their books within just a couple weeks, too.

Using the Publish & Profit model, these successful authors learned to ask the right questions. Let me explain where most people get hung up and never make any progress, whether it's writing a book, doing marketing or just being an effective business owner because they're asking the *wrong* questions like:

- What software should I use to format my Kindle book?
- Where can I find an editor if I'm not good at writing?
- How do I find a designer to create my book cover?

We have answers to every one of those questions and more, but most people ask questions in the wrong order. These are "HOW-TO" QUESTIONS. To be effective, first, we have to answer the "WHAT" and the "WHY."

"How" questions cause most people to get overwhelmed, freeze up, become indecisive and procrastinate. Once you have the "why" and "what" figured out, your book becomes a mission. The how is the easy part.

After writing nine books in less than three years and helping nearly 500 people become successful authors, the folks I speak to who don't finish or aren't successful are the ones who obsess over all the "how to" nonsense. For now don't worry about that unless you want to fall into the trap of procrastination and failure.

It's really important that you get connected to the "who" - your reader, get fully connected with their hopes, dreams, passions, curiosities and fears. Because once you do this, the "how" questions melt away because you get connected and attached to your mission of helping these people and making a difference.

My friend Tony Robbins says, "The quality of our lives is directly proportional to the quality of the questions we ask." When you ask quality questions, you get quality answers—the kind that can fuel your income like a rocket powered racecar.

According to a survey published in the *New York Times*, 81% of the 313 million people in the US want to write a book someday. That's 254 million. Imagine how many people worldwide long to express themselves through a book? (And as a "by the way", imagine the size of the consulting market to write books for business people).

How many of the 254 million do you think have actually written and published a book?

According to a recent article in *Forbes Magazine*, about 600,000 to 1 million every year.

It's a mere 0.3%

I think that's sad… and I believe it stems from inaction and asking the wrong questions.

If you have never published a book… or you have and you're not happy with the results, there is a reason… and it's a reason we can fix before the end of this chapter.

This entire book is ALL ABOUT the stuff that matters most. It's about psychology, not technology. It's about mindset over matter.

Let me give you two great questions to give you clarity, vision and your much needed "WHY."

1. The FIRST high-quality question to ask is: **WHO is my book for? Or, more important, WHY will someone BUY my book?**

    We'll answer that question in a moment.
2. The SECOND high-quality question to ask is: **HOW will my books make me money, grow my list, platform, brand or business?**

That's what the next chapter is all about—the top 10 reasons to write a book, even if you aren't a writer.

Once you understand the "WHAT," the "HOW" questions begin to answer themselves. The whole process gets really easy - because once you connect with the WHO and the WHAT, the process gets super easy...writing your book feels like you're speaking on the phone with an old friend, your mom, dad, spouse or child.

WATCH FIVE WAYS A BOOK WILL BUILD YOUR BUSINESS

You'll notice every chapter in this book includes a "CTA" (call to action) which is designed to give you a reason to learn more and build an online relationship with you.

My goal is to teach you several strategies you can use in your book to do the same. I've prepared several training videos that will show you a variety of ways you can get attention, build a prospect list and get your foot in the door with practically anyone quickly and easily.

This has worked for hundreds of my past clients and customers in over 60 countries and multiple languages and I know it can work for you too.

Visit www.PublishAndProfit.com/BookBonus
or text your email address to (858) 707-7417

CHAPTER FOUR

The Top 10 Reasons to Write a Book (Even if You Aren't a Writer)

"I want to do something splendid...Something heroic or wonderful that won't be forgotten after I'm dead... I think I shall write books."

Louisa May Alcott

Grab a pen and circle the "reasons to write a book" in the next few pages that resonate with you. I'm a huge believer in taking notes the "old fashioned way" with a pencil or pen, especially when I'm dreaming big.

Remember, we're going after your "BIG WHY" right now; the reason you're going to write and publish a book in the first place - and who you're going to help with your book.

Reason #1: A book is an instant credibility booster for you and your business

It's positioning and authority wrapped in a paper wrapper. Think about it—don't you treat someone a little differently when you find out they're a bestselling author? You'll be amazed how many people want you to autograph your book for them; and unlike a business card, books don't get thrown away.

Inside your book, you can demonstrate your genius, show examples and social proof of your knowledge, wisdom and experience without being a braggart. You're treated very differently—with celebrity status. It's like getting an exclusive VIP ticket to a private members-only club.... past the velvet rope to access a community that enables your freedom and autonomy; and when people introduce you to someone else, they feel special when they announce you as an author; or, better yet, as a "#1 bestselling author."

Reason #2: A book creates the ultimate foot in the door strategy

For a couple of bucks, you can mail your book to a prospect to get your foot in the door… but here's another little strategy I use to bypass the gatekeepers. I buy my own books on Amazon and have them delivered to a prospect, gift-wrapped, with a card… and Amazon PAYS ME a royalty when I buy my own books!

When is the last time you ignored a package from Amazon, especially one that is gift-wrapped? I don't know about you, but I would consider it very rude if my assistant opened up my presents!

People "meet" you in your book. You start a one-way conversation with them. You reveal your "reason why" you do what do you in your book… which creates a reason why they're going to do business with you.

Recently, I was invited to meet with a billionaire who had read two of my books. We met at a very fancy hotel in Beverly Hills. I didn't have to spend ANY time talking about me, what I did, why I did it or my background. We just got right down to business; and because I already had credibility, positioning and authority because of my book, I wasn't competing with anyone else. It was just a matter of discussing the terms, timeline and price.

Now, I'm not saying you're going to get calls from billionaires as soon as you write your book (even though Andy Falco did a deal with the country of Bahrain because of his book), but you certainly can start talking to millionaire business owners and get invited into their offices to meet with CEOs and other VIPs.

Reason #3: Use your book to get traffic, generate leads and build your list

Getting and keeping customers is the holy grail of every business. BOOKS are one the lowest cost ways to generate high-quality leads.

Here's how it works:

Every chapter in your book tells a short story and answers a question. Your book is a library filled with social proof, examples, stories and ways to show you care, know what you're talking about and can help the reader solve just about any challenge. Throughout the book, you invite the reader to visit a web page where they enter their contact information, text their email address to a phone number, or call and leave their name and information.

Each "call-to-action" is a way to interactively engage the reader and drive them to some kind of bonus or gift. You can give away training videos, a free audiobook, surveys, trials of your products or services, a consulting session, diagnostics or a high-value way to get closer and deepen the relationship.

In our experience, for every 10 books sold on Amazon, we get 2-4 leads. Think about it. You're not only going getting paid every time you sell a book, you're getting leads too. In the "Promote" chapter, you'll see exactly how it's done.

For example, in one of my books, I wrote about how a video shot with an iPhone was virtually indistinguishable from that of a professional $4,000 DSLR video camera with a $1,000 lens except by video professionals. I made the point that you have a video production studio in your pocket. I told the reader to text their email address to watch a side-by-side demo. And, as a result, I got their email address and phone number and generated tens of thousands of dollars in sales.

The reason you do embed a "Call To Action" in your book is because publishers don't give you the contact information of the book buyer. You need the right strategies, tools and systems to drive readers to your offers and capture leads.

Remember I told you that when you ask the right "WHY" questions, you eventually come to the "HOW"? What I just showed you is a good example of that.

By asking the right questions, you get the right answers.

I just mentioned lead capture and email or phone follow up. And the moment I said that, you probably asked a "HOW" question about what kind of software or system to use to make that happen. Here is the answer:

In our system, we have "Marketing Machines"—they are tools that sell books, capture leads, follow up and automate everything for you… and most of the copy is already written for you.

You literally fill in the blanks, press a button and in less than 10 minutes, you have a full website that sells books, collects leads, follows up and delivers content with email, mobile text, voicemail… and even sell your products! Better yet, we have a team that does it with you.

You don't need to be a techie, hire a marketing team or get bogged down in details. We've already done that for you.

You'll notice every chapter in this book does the exact same thing - there's a reason and an opportunity to "go deeper" to get value and learn more, experience this book interactively, with videos, an opportunity to join me for an interactive online "webcast" where you can ask questions, meet people in our awesome community who help each other brainstorm book ideas, titles, provide book cover feedback, buy each other's books and often do business together too.

That's the "how"... that's easy.

For now, stay focused on the "why"—and being CREATIVE.

You can teach without selling or being salesy.

Reason #4: Books sell your products and services faster and easier

Your book can talk about what you do, who you do it for, include case studies and results and invite the reader to try them out.

For example, if you are a chiropractor, a fitness instructor or in pain management, you can demonstrate three different stretches or exercises to eliminate neck or back pain. If you are a nutritionist or dietitian, you could discuss the benefits of using coconut oil in a cooking demonstration. By demonstrating your product or service and talking about the benefits and showing proof it works, you multiply your sales when you include a "CTA" (Call to Action) in your book and capture leads with text messaging, mobile-responsive websites, QR codes, voicemail or shortcodes.

My own doctor, Nalini Chilkov, wrote her book *32 Ways to Outsmart Cancer* based on her years of expertise. She became a #1 bestseller in three categories in less than a day... and now she has the title "#1 Bestselling Author" for life!

So instead of spending hours answering the same questions that she's been answering for the past 15 years about health and cancer, she can get right down to business and solve her patient's health challenges because THEY ASK GREAT QUESTIONS after reading her book. The result is happier clients and customers and more money in less time for you!

Reason #5: A book is a perfect way to position yourself as a consultant or authority

This one is brain-dead simple.

Who would you rather do business with: a coach, consultant, doctor, nutritionist, financial planner, fitness expert, therapist or mechanic who hands you a business card that says "I am a Self Proclaimed Expert - Hire me!" on it.

OR

A professional who's a #1 bestselling author and hands you a book about the problem you want to fix - and autographs it for you with their mobile phone number and email address?

Who are you going to remember? Who are you more likely to do business with? Do you lose or throw away business cards? How often do you lose or throw away an autographed book?

Here's a story about one of our clients, Everett O'Keefe. He does mobile marketing, video and social media marketing for small business owners. He was struggling and barely scraping by selling his services for $80 per month in a very competitive environment. Everett is married has three young children to provide for.

Everett wrote a book called *The Video Tractor Beam* and in less than 30 days, he published, promoted and became a #1 bestseller with our proven system.

All of a sudden, out of the blue, he started getting noticed. People would say, "I hear you're a bestselling author;" another guy walked up and said, "Aren't you kind of a big deal?"

He decided if he could write a book for himself, he could definitely do it for others. Soon he had people approaching him, asking him if he would help them write, publish, promote and become bestselling authors too. Now he and some of our other clients are charging as much as $20,000 to write, publish and promote books for clients as a service.

In fact, Everett met some of his first customers at our live events, like Blair Bernhardt, who had a plan that could help save America's crumbling roads and preserve America's infrastructure. The result? *The Book on Better Roads: Saving Your Crumbling Roads with Practical Pavement Management.*

Everett went on to write, publish and promote a total of eight books and a CD for a church that made it to the Billboard Top 50. The same strategies used to publish and promote books works for music, spoken word and practically anything you sell or promote online! This is a totally integrated blueprint!

Because Everett is a devout Christian, he's been finding it very easy to find like-minded clients and customers who share his values and beliefs! Publishing books for yourself and others gives you a purpose-driven life and more meaning.

You'll meet Everett O'Keefe and hear more about his story in an upcoming chapter and you'll also meet some of our certified consultants who use our systems to start their own profitable publishing and marketing businesses part-time and full-time... and many of them have no prior marketing or publishing experience!

Reason #6: Writing books is a great way to get speaking opportunities

My friend Ed Rush started an online marketing business that helped attorneys get more clients. The biggest problem he had was getting his foot in the door to even talk to the attorneys. On multiple occasions, he tried to speak through bar associations; but the problem was, they weren't going to let him just walk in and pitch his services because he didn't have the credibility, positioning or authority as a "Legal Marketing Expert."

After making dozens of calls, he had no bookings; not even a response. That's when he wrote his book, *How to Turn Clicks Into Clients - The Ultimate Law Firm Guide for Getting More Clients Through the Internet.* When he called to speak to the director of training and special events for the Palo Alto bar association and told them he was a bestselling author of a book about marketing for attorneys, he immediately got booked as a headline presenter. He and his partners went on to get 47 more speaking events in that very same year. Because of the book, 97% of the attendees gave Ed their contact info because they wanted to work with Ed and his team. Each deal was worth between $5,000 – $15,000; and it's a high six-figure-per-year business… all because of a book.

Here's another example.

When an event promoter in the medical tourism industry wanted to hire a speaker to talk about "word-of-mouth marketing," she searched on Amazon for books on the topic. One of our customers, John Cote got the call because he had written *Mobilize Your Customers* and used our system to rank high online. From the speaking gig, he was inspired to start a podcast about Medical Tourism, because there was no competition and high demand for that topic.

After only five months, his podcast not only became #1 in the health category on iTunes, he reached over 100,000 downloads a month. Doctors and hospitals are hiring him to do their marketing for them - from all over the world! Better yet, he was asked to speak again at their next event!

He repurposed his best podcasts and transcribed them into a new book, *Healthcare Elsewhere: Inspiring Medical Tourism Success Stories, What You Can Learn from These 21 People Who Got Their Medical Care Abroad That Will Save You Money, Time and Quite Possibly Your Life*. The book will be used to generate leads and business. John is not only a bestselling author and an international marketing consultant, but he also has a hugely popular niche podcast and advertisers and sponsors are competing against each other to advertise on his show!

Do you see how a book can generate multiple streams of income and create huge opportunities for you?

It's about "wrapping a book around your business" or "how to wrap a new business idea you might have around a book…"

Reason #7: Your book is a perfect way to get media attention, radio shows, TV interviews and traction in social media

Every chapter in your book can easily become the subject of a TV or radio interview, a speech, a social media post, a YouTube video or a podcast episode. The book becomes a "marketing roadmap" for your messaging and marketing. It gives you a script and a formula for what to speak about and share.

It eliminates doubt and confusion; interviewers and hosts will pick the topics they want you to talk about based on what's in the book, which makes it super easy for you to just show up and be the expert you already are.

For example, one of our members, Andy Broadaway, used this system to write and publish his book, *Top Ten YouTube Mistakes and What You Can Learn from them to Create Profits*. It quickly shot up to a #1 bestseller. A radio show producer from NBC news radio KCAA met Andy at "YouTube Space" in LA, and when Andy mentioned his book was #1, he got booked on the radio program for a 20 minute segment!

After his appearance on the show, Andy's book remained a #1 bestseller for five consecutive days and they asked him back on the show!

Remember Sandi Masori, the balloon artist? She used our system, wrote three books in less than 30 days each, and ended up on *The Today Show*.

She has a business that involves creating trade show exhibits and event stages with balloons. Now that she's been on TV and is a #1 bestselling author, do you think she has any problem getting her foot in the door with event promoters and trade show executives?

One word. Two letters. *No*.

Reason #8: A book can build or grow any local business

I talk to LOTS of local business owners who tell me they don't understand why they should write a book or what it will do for them. They think that because they only do business in a specific town, region or neighborhood, a book won't make a difference to their bottom line.

Think again.

For example, Dave Bell has been in the pest control business for 40 years. He didn't think a book made sense for his business.

I asked him 4 simple questions:

- Do you ever fight for business with competitors?
- Do you have any trouble standing out in the crowd?
- Do you ever get asked the same questions over and over again from your prospects?
- Do you get price resistance or thre?

Dave said yes to every one, and he accepted my challenge about writing a book. So, he just sat down, answered the top 20 questions prospects asked him about getting rid of ants, roaches and other nasty things and started his first book. It's called, *Things That Crawl in the Night: Life Without Bugs. He already had all the content – and has been answering the same questions for almost 20 years.* Most of the content was already on his web site in the form of FAQs.

Now he has something that's really high quality to give away to his prospects; instead of a sales letter or website, he will stand out way beyond his competitors who don't have books. Bestseller status gives you immediate credibility and authority and positions you as a go-to person.

The fact is, this works for any business; anywhere in the world. Thinking you're "local" is absolutely irrelevant as to whether or not a book we be a powerful marketing tool for you.

Reason #9: Marketing in heavily regulated industries is easier

Businesses like financial planning, investing, medical, healthcare, franchises, stocks and trading, legal, fitness or multilevel marketing are easy (and legal) to market with books.

Many of our customers believed for years they couldn't write a book to market a business, because legal teams and compliance departments would stop them. However, with very few exceptions, no company can prevent you from sharing your *personal life experiences, stories, and topical or general advice.*

For example, Frank Leyes is a financial planner who talked for years about writing a book but let compliance worries and excuses stand in his way. Once he realized they were just excuses, he had a breakthrough, sat down and quickly wrote his book, *The Way of Wealth: 7 Steps To Financial Freedom In A World Of Economic Dependence.* With our proven system and by leveraging our community, his book shot up to a #1 bestseller in 24 hours —in three different categories.

Now Frank uses his book to get speaking gigs. At his most recent one, he spoke in front of a group of 300 financial advisors. He used our tools to capture leads and build a list while he spoke. He then mailed a video to that list; and five advisors signed up for a mastermind event and paid him $3,600 each. That's $18,000. Not too bad for his first event!

Because of his book, Frank's revenue is up over $100,000 from last year. He's booked seven full fee speaking engagements for $5,500 to $7,000 each, plus expenses, and he's got a five-figure consulting contract.

Once again, this strategy will work for any business.

A book just gives people a reason to listen to you and take you seriously, faster.

And a BIG *by the way*: when you use our system to start a consulting business like our certified consultants have—to write, publish and promote books for clients—THIS is the market to go after.

Reason #10: Published authors make more money and help more people

I could spend days sharing personal success stories from hundreds of our customers and what their books have done for them. In fact, you'll meet several of them in the next chapter. Many have seen results in as little as a week after they publish their book.

Your book is about gaining access to an exclusive, member's only club; meeting with CEOs and celebrities; getting VIP treatment; gaining instant credibility, garnering speaking opportunities and attracting media attention. It's about getting paid what you're worth, not what you can get.

More impact, more income.

Clarity and confidence.

A clear roadmap for your marketing and promotion.

A way to become competition and recession-proof.

You can do this for other people as a service—like many of our certified consultants - who regularly get paid between $2,000 and $15,000 or more to help people publish and promote books.

It's an opportunity to make more, live more and give more.

You get huge partners like Amazon, Apple, Barnes and Noble and about a half dozen more who sell your books and pay you 70% commissions and sometimes even more. But that's not all; they also each give you a personal author website that gives you high-value SEO ranking credibility and the equivalent of an Amazon and Apple endorsement. They give you a place to post your social media link, book signing and event schedules, as well as a gallery for pictures and videos of you with your books, your clients, customers and television appearances.

It's social proof… and it's free.

So when you ask the question, "HOW WILL A BOOK GROW MY BUSINESS?" All the things I just shared with you should make that very obvious.

But let's get into some of the "HOW." The most effective books are those that tell stories of transformation. First, you begin with your own story of *why* you do what you do; how you've used your system to help yourself, a family member or your clients and customers; how it made you and them feel. The more emotional your book is, the more it will connect with your reader.

We call this "mess to success" - it's a simple before and after story. It makes you accessible, approachable, more human and establishes empathy between you and your reader.

The two big mistakes people make when they write unsuccessful books is that a) it's a bunch of facts and b) they think the book has to be perfect and long to get results.

That's not only a recipe for disaster; it's a *boring* disaster. Very few people have the time, patience, and attention span or desire to read a 1,000 page tell-all book especially from a first-time author. Once you understand the next two concepts, you'll not only grab your audience by the eyeballs, you'll keep them.

Inside you right now are dozens, maybe even hundreds of stories. When you share heartfelt, authentic, emotional stories from your unique perspective when combined with details, those are 10 times more effective in connecting with your reader than facts and figures.

When you go through one of the guided exercises in our system, most people learn they have 4-5 books inside them but they just didn't know how to get them out. It's not hard—you already do it every day when you talk to clients, customers, prospects, and friends.

It only takes about a half day to produce enough content for a 120-140 page book.

That should have answered the typical question I get which is: WHAT WILL I PUT IN MY BOOK? So many of our friends and members come to us screaming, "I'm not a writer!"

You don't have to be.

You're a storyteller.

You're in the ATTENTION business.

You're in SHOW business.

If you're wondering:

- *WHO WILL BUY my book?*
- *WHO WILL LISTEN TO ME?*
- *WHO WILL CARE?*
- *Who am I anyway?*
- *I'm not the authority!*

Those are just mind tricks that your brain and your fears are playing on you. Let me share a secret with you: this is called *imposter syndrome.* Everyone has it—including the biggest celebrities the world.

Many people never get past imposter syndrome. They become frozen in place and never take advantage of the opportunity that's in front of them right now: to get marketed, distributed and have your book sold by the biggest brands in the world and get paid.

The next big secret once you get past the content question or concern is becoming attractive to your target audience - and looking like a celebrity.

The secret to that is PACKAGING. It's a beautiful book cover – and you can have one made for as little as $5.

We give things a lot more value when they're in an attractive or pretty package. People really do judge a book by its cover. It's basic psychology.

In addition to a beautiful book cover, you need a great book title and descriptive subtitle that's designed to get attention, GRAB a prospect and sell your book.

In an upcoming chapter, you'll be guided through a step-by-step process, actually a formula that you can use to quickly come up with an attention-getting, results-driven book title, subtitle and cover exercise.

CHAPTER FIVE

The New Integrated Hybrid Publishing Model

---

*"You have to learn the rules of the game.
And then you have to play better than anyone else."*

Albert Einstein

This quote is appropriate for this chapter because lots of people talk about a "dying publishing industry" and how traditional publishing is going the way of the dinosaur.

There are actually more books being written, distributed and sold today than ever before and those numbers increase every year. The business has radically changed, but there's room for both models.

That's why we call the Publish and Profit system a "New, Integrated Hybrid Publishing Model"—because both worlds can peacefully co-exist and as an author, you can leverage both to make more money and have significantly more impact at the same time.

If you are an existing author or want to get a publishing deal someday with a major publishing house, then you're really going to enjoy this chapter.

When we did our pilot test of the Publish and Profit Training Program with our 39 customers, we invited two top New York literary agents, Celeste Fine and Scott Hoffman to attend and speak at the event.

Both Celeste and Scott are known in the industry as being open-minded, conscious and aware of the massive changes that have been occurring in the traditional publishing world that many old school publishers are very afraid of. They're also well-respected and known for getting their clients high six-figure and seven-figure book publishing deals.

One of Celeste's clients, for example, is my friend JJ Virgin, author of *The Virgin Diet* and *Virgin Diet Cookbook* (both *New York Times* best sellers). In traditional publishing, the business cycle usually takes 18 to 36 months—from the time the author has an idea, writes a book proposal, gets it accepted by a traditional publisher, writes the book, creates the marketing, the artwork, and the book cover, until the book gets launched into distribution and retail stores.

The biggest challenge that "old school" publishers have these days is that the cycle of publishing is actually quite long. It is, however, still a practical, usable and useful model, because of the volume of books that get sold through retail when you've established yourself as a viable brand and are properly prepared. And when they publish and promote a best-selling author, everyone can make a lot of money.

In traditional publishing, the author generally gets 7% - 15% of the sales of the books after expenses. That doesn't sound like a lot, and if the book doesn't sell well, it isn't. However, the publisher is betting on the author and they are very careful and selective about whom they choose to work with. These days, it's almost impossible to get a traditional book deal unless you have a substantial email database of 80,000 to 250,000 or more people who are active and engaged, and an extremely large social media presence including Facebook, Twitter, LinkedIn, and other users. In other words, you need to have what is known as a "platform" in the industry. You need to be known for something specific in your industry, be well-respected, be media trained, have experience being on the radio, television, in the news, media, and conducting interviews.

To someone just starting out, the thought of this is justifiably overwhelming and many people see the troubling "chicken and the egg" problem and wonder "how in the heck can I just get started?"

Traditional publishers bet on a "winning horse." In the past, they *advance* the author tens or hundreds of thousands of dollars, or in some cases, millions of dollars in order to attract that author to work with them. Due to the nature and complexity of their business, a publisher's internal overhead costs are extremely high. They have to make a lot of money in order to be profitable, and they take and make big gambles on top authors.

It's really no different from the movie industry. When a movie has Tom Cruise in it, they know they're going to make several hundred million dollars. That's why they pay him tens of millions to be in the movie. It's an almost guaranteed return on investment when you have the *right talent that's recognizable, memorable and proven to deliver results.* The majority of actors struggle and have day jobs!

Literary agents who sell deals to the publishers get paid 15% of whatever the author makes, so a deal has to be big enough to cover their overhead and expenses too. 15% of $100,000 is $15,000—and if that's for 18-36 months of work, an agent needs a lot of clients to make a decent living or have some big names on their roster.

15% of $500,000 is $75,000. That makes more sense, if you have 5-10 big authors as clients. The reality is that most agents have to work through thousands of proposals and make hundreds of pitches to build a roster of top authors to make good money.

Publishing has been and still is a very big business. However, now that Amazon is responsible for what is quickly approaching 40% of all book sales worldwide, traditional publishers face major competition, as well as the challenge that any author can publish his or her book in days or weeks instead of years, and keep all the money.

No agent required - that's the "Publish and Profit" model. Author writes book, publishes, promotes and keeps all the money.

It can be done in a few weeks and if the author knows how to market himself or herself and can sell products or services as a "backend," they can make a great living. That's what I do - and what I teach other people to do.

To the outsider who might not understand all of these models, it may seem as though traditional publishing is going to go away, but that simply isn't the case. A publisher cultivates talent and knows the retail business extremely well and it's still HUGE. Most authors don't understand how to name or package their books, create great book covers that get attention and understand the nuances of getting books placed inside traditional retail establishments.

Amazon isn't going to do that for you.

Why should any of this matter to you, and why should you care?

There are a few reasons. First, there is a strategy for using both models extremely effectively. Second, a traditionally published author can use self-publishing and the Publish and Profit integrated model very effectively. If you are a first-time author, understanding how the business works means that at some point, if you build enough of an audience, or what the industry calls a "platform", you could get a sizeable advance in the future for yourself, and benefit from everything that goes along with that.

You can become a "Tom Cruise" in your niche or topic, build a following, fan base, grow your list on the back of Amazon, Apple, Google, YouTube, attract a massive social audience, start a podcast, get your "backend" products and services made and start making hundreds of thousands or millions of dollars.

And once you have a following, the big players will come to you.

Agents and publishers in the business of spotting talent just like movie and sports agents.

Only now, you can build a platform much more quickly: 6-18 months is possible although 2-3 years is more realistic. I've been studying and practicing this process for over 15 years, I know I could start all over from scratch and get to where I am in 9-18 months.

If your goal is to just use your book to grow your local business, consulting services, get your foot in the door or be a fancy business card, you don't need "a platform." I've seen hundreds of my clients become local or niche celebrities in a matter of 2-3 months once they publish their book.

It's my opinion that if you start with this knowledge, you can become an authority, build momentum and create an international presence with some subtle "tweaks" and nuances and set yourself up for a big payday when you implement the strategies in this book.

You can use the Publish & Profit model to rapidly write, publish, and promote your books, build an audience, grow your business, and eventually sign with a traditional literary agent who can help you get a sizeable six or seven-figure advance. This in turn can dramatically increase your authority, visibility, and value in any industry, and help you get on big network television, and gain major "celebrity association" in your industry and worldwide.

If you are already a traditionally-published author, you can write, publish, and promote self-published books between your 18 to 36-month traditional publishing cycles so that you will continue to stay in the media, remain relevant, continue a conversation with your existing base of prospects and customers, as well as leverage social media, Amazon, and other distribution platforms to build your list and drive additional traffic leads and sales to your present business.

Nothing beats frequency and "new" – the infrequent publishing cycle is obsolete.

Here's an even bigger idea.

If you are a traditionally-published author or an integrated, hybrid published author, or a brand new author, this model allows you to test and try out your ideas, build an audience, and grow your list with zero risk and have total control over your content and "IP" (intellectual property).

To you, the author, your objective and goal is to be seen, heard, read, and viewed anytime anywhere on any device. We also call this the *You Everywhere Now philosophy*, and any time your book is being read or placed in the hands or on a device of your target prospect, you benefit - especially when the reader converts into an active member of your list.

If you can spend 18 to 36 months producing several books, creating a following and platform, building a list, engaging with your prospects and customers, and growing your business, you can then sign up with a traditional literary agent who helps you get a six or seven-figure advance. As far as I'm concerned, that's "free" money.

If you are a traditionally published author who has several books that are already published, you can use this model to either re-launch or re-release those books if you have control over those properties. Or you could easily create derivative works or additional books on or around that same idea or topic and extend your platform and your visibility.

Here's an example of something my friend, JJ Virgin, *New York Times* bestselling author is doing right now with this model.

JJ has recently been awarded a multiple seven-figure deal for two of her books. Her traditional publishing cycle is about 18 months. She is appearing on a PBS special that is branded *The Sugar Impact Diet that is* consistent with her books. The show will increase visibility for her, her book and her products. She wins, the publisher wins and PBS wins due to the combined momentum and visibility of these things working in concert with one another.

Her publisher will not be interested in small "niche" books. For example, they probably won't pay her a big advance for a cookbook that's just for diabetics or a smoothie recipe cookbook because there isn't enough of an audience for a narrowly focused book. It isn't financially feasible for them to get behind or promote. But for JJ, she can easily create a book a month, self-publish it, remain visible and relevant in the media, and use those books to promote her existing and traditionally-published books, drive traffic, leads and sales to her websites, sell more nutritional supplements, energy and snack bars, and shakes, which is what her real business revolves around - and how she makes money.

And while that happens, those "niche books" can keep her in the media and attract new buyers to her traditionally published books.

New is good. New every month or two is even better. A ravenous tribe will buy everything you make and it's often much harder to restart momentum once it's lost than it is to start from scratch.

The Publish and Profit Integrated Hybrid Publishing Model is compatible with both worlds. They don't compete but they complement each other, and the publishers, the distributors, the readers, and the authors, all benefit equally.

CHAPTER SIX

Step #1–Prepare

"If you don't design your own life plan, chances are you'll fall into someone else's plan.
And guess what they have planned for you? Not much."

Jim Rohn

You can't paint a house until you build it; you can't publish, promote or profit from your book until you do some prep work first.

There are seven steps in the preparation process:

1. Figuring out your "Big Why"
2. Choosing your audience
3. Your title and subtitle
4. Your book cover
5. Your hook
6. The actual content
7. Mindset and establishing a deadline.

Let's begin with your "Big Why."

One of the major reasons most people never actually start or finish their book is because they don't understand what their "Big Why" is. In order to understand what their "Big Why" is, they really have to dig deep and understand what their unique story is. In my experience, most people's unique story is tied to their greatest pain—something they've tried to overcome most their life. It explains the reason why they do what they do for the people whom they serve.

For example, my wife, Vivian, is Jewish and her parents are Holocaust survivors. Growing up, she had a great deal of pain associated with the loss of the majority of her family. She only has a couple of relatives that she ever knew or met, because most of them were killed in Yugoslavia, where her parents are from. Her parents barely escaped with their lives when Nazis were marching into Yugoslavia. They jumped into a tiny boat and went from Yugoslavia to Bari, Italy where they were refugees for several years until they had an opportunity to emigrate to the United States.

Her father struggled. He came from a very wealthy family and he was an opera singer. At some point, his voice "broke" and he could no longer sing. He struggled finding work and became addicted to alcohol and drugs.

In the 1950's and 1960's there were very few social services available to help people with these types of challenges. He beat and abused Vivian and her two brothers and her mother. He sexually molested her from the time she was four until she was fourteen years old.

After doing an enormous amount of personal development and inner work and healing her emotional wounds for decades, she started helping children and women in Uganda and created a non-profit foundation, The Just Like My Child Foundation (www.JustLikeMyChild.org).

While she was in Africa, she started working with young girls and women. At one point, she was talking to a group of about 20 girls, all between the ages of nine and eleven, and decided to ask those girls if they had ever been sexually molested or abused. *Every single one* of them raised their hands. It was that moment when Vivian became absolutely committed to what her "Big Why," her vision and her mission was because she knew exactly how they felt. This experience became a massive driver and has helped her raise millions of dollars and prevent thousands of other girls from meeting that same fate.

Vivian realized she has to tell stories to raise money. Her "Big Why" helps her bring attention to the cause and because she's emotionally connected through a shared story. People recognize and feel it when they meet her.

Her "Big Why" helps her develop videos, content, media articles, presentations and an event to fundraise and bring awareness to what it is she is doing.

Her greatest pain, greatest shame, and biggest fears have given her the salvation and strength that is changing and saving lives.

You, me—everyone—has a story and a "Big Why", that when it's told through a book, can captivate and connect with your ideal target audience.

And yes, this works in business too.

Here's an example of my "Big Why"—and I have more than one.

I grew up in a lower middle-income home and I was a failure in school. I barely passed high school and never learned how to learn because I am ADHD and a kinesthetic learner. In other words, I need to "do" in an immersive environment in order to learn. I am constantly active and busy. It's hard for me to sit still for an extended period of time.

When I was growing up, I felt alien and isolated and didn't like the fact that I didn't have resources or tools or access to technology because we didn't have money. The day I turned 16, I worked full time and started businesses because I wanted to become a millionaire - I thought that would change everything (ha!).

My "Big Why" and my pain had to do with never wanting to be poor or be "stuck" without resources. Fortunately, I have been able to successfully communicate some of my pain in a way that attracted entrepreneurs to our businesses and services. Many entrepreneurs come from a background similar to mine. I understand the plight of the struggling or startup entrepreneur and have made a good living creating products and services that helped them build their businesses by getting more traffic, leads and sales with video, social media, mobile, email and content marketing.

I made my products for *me*. Then I told my story in a way they relate to. People relate to you through your stories and your "Big Why."

Discovering yours is as simple as asking yourself "Why do I do what I do? And, how does that help you empathize and attract my ideal customer to your business?"

Dig deep. If you're struggling right now with this, don't beat yourself up. It may take a little while to connect with the source. But once you discover what it is and can articulate it in an authentic, connected way, you'll find more people trust you and connect with your message.

The biggest challenge I see in authors who are just starting out is that they don't understand why they do what they do, they don't understand who they serve, or who their audience really is. There is a simple shortcut to getting to the core of this and that is understanding what your unique story is and tying that to your "Big Why."

The simple strategy is to get clear on *why* you love what you love, what you are passionate about and why, and have a clear understanding of who you best serve and what your value is.

CHAPTER SEVEN

Who Is Your Book For?

"Success is about creating benefit for all and enjoying the process. If you focus on this & adopt this definition, success is yours."

Kelly Kim

An avatar is a representative character your book or product is designed for. Once you know who your avatar is, it's easy to establish a message that will appeal to this person. And once you clarify the avatar and message and start sharing this message, you'll attract this type of person into your business.

Let me describe to you my avatar and "perfect customer". Her name is Lori.

Lori is a successful radiologist who lives in Austin, Texas. When you first meet her, she comes across as a smart, low-key woman with entrepreneurial ambitions. She's dreamed for years of being a bestselling author, developing products that cross over between personal development and medicine and building an online business that makes money while she sleeps. Lori's CV (Curriculum Vitae) is 1.5 inches thick—she's an incredible student, she's published hundreds of medical papers, is incredibly successful and excels at everything she focuses on.

Her husband, Steven, is a high school teacher who is a passionate scuba diving instructor. Their son, Richard, is a smart student who enjoys theater and is attending his second year of college. One of their favorite family holiday pastimes is watching *Muppet movies* together. I love their innocence, empathy and compassion for each other as a family.

Lori, Steven and Richard have attended my live events as a family. They operate with the highest degree of respect for each other and Lori and Steven are like high school kids who just fell madly in love with each other. Lori still blushes when Steven looks at her. Last time I was in Austin, Texas, they took me out for dinner at a fabulous restaurant.

When I write scripts to sell my products and services and even when I write my books, I write to Lori and imagine Steven and Richard are sitting with her together as a family.

It's easy to write for Lori when I know about who she is, what she loves, what's important to her and what her goals and aspirations are.

Over the past few years, I've been attracting more "entrepreneurial families" and "entrepreneurial professionals" to my tribe. They're perfect customers and clients. Lori implements and gets results. I genuinely love them as people—and as dear friends.

And as an added bonus, Lori is the first person to invest in every product I create. When she's excited about "the next big thing," I know I have a winner on my hands.

Why do I share this story with you?

Lori (and her family) is my primary book and business avatars (the ideal customer persona for my business). I want more customers and clients *just like them*. I want more families to write books, create products and start businesses. It's incredibly satisfying to see an entire family attend my live events – and to my private consulting sessions.

The real secret to writing a successful book and having a successful business understands <u>clearly</u> who your perfect customer is. When you write or speak to "the one," more like them are attracted to your message and connect with you. They frequently say things to you like, "I don't know how you do it, but it's as though you were talking to me in your video or your books feels as though you wrote it to me." That's because *I do.*

Now - the next few points I make will sound harsh and that's for a reason. I do so unapologetically and because if you really, really get this, it'll save you years of frustration, wasted time, energy and money.

If you want to know who I DON'T write for - just look at a couple of the negative reviews of my books on Amazon. It's pretty obvious and apparent in the tone of how they write - you feel the *anger and bite* in the way they communicate. They're usually haters, trolls and a-holes. Just look at the other reviews they write. They're filled with the same *vitriol.* I say this not to be "right" or to make them "wrong". Some of them just won't like the way you or I write. I share this with you because once you are visibly successful, you'll find jealous, angry, hateful people crawl out of dark holes and project their anger and self-hatred on *you.* My advice is to completely ignore them and focus on the people you care about, love and those who resonate with your message.

Losers and haters aren't buyers. Focus all of your energy appealing to the 50-80 percent that appreciate your message and content. You're writing to your lovers, not haters.

Over the past 20 years, after studying the most successful and prolific writers and marketers in the world, I've found the best ones are incredibly empathic, compassionate people—even if their exteriors are "hard." They "feel" their target audience when they write. They write as though they are writing to YOU or me. You feel like you've found a friend who understands you.

Assuming your objective in your book is to create a deep, trusting connection and bond with your reader, you'll use the strategies we'll cover later in this book to engage with them beyond the pages of your book and find a way to bring them to your audio book, videos, website, social media site, a diagnostic tool, consultation, phone call or event and move them towards a sale and doing business with you.

I've met thousands of struggling entrepreneurs that are unsuccessful selling their products and their services. When I ask them, "Who is your perfect customer? Will you please share a story of transformation," most of them can't do it. Or they say, "Everyone is my customer."

BZZZZZZTTTTT! WRONG ANSWER!

If I were to ask you to tell me a story of one person, who you have successfully helped, who implemented what you told them to do, they paid you, they got results, and you were able to communicate clearly what it was you did for them and what those results were, then you're on the right track. That's whom you write about and to.

A book is a conversation between you and "The One."

Unsuccessful entrepreneurs, corporate leaders and authors who talk in general terms or can't focus on a single individual customer are the ones who struggle the most. They write to "everyone" and attract nobody, or they attract crazy people who are confused, schizophrenic, desperate *psychic vampires* that make running and owning a business not fun, and they tax your support network and employees.

They're usually broke and looking for a quick fix, the easy way out or a solution with a "magic button." In other words, they expect something for nothing. They're almost always where they are because they can't focus on what they really want or need. And if they don't find the magic unicorn that poop gold bricks from your books and products, they'll blame you for their misery. 99% of them are broke because they've been practicing broke behavior for decades and come from a scarcity mindset.

If you focus your energy, resources or money on trying to fix broken, broke, angry, whiny, losers, you're going to go broke and your high-quality prospects and customers are going to avoid you. Focus first on becoming wealthy and give your money away to a charity to fix broken people if that's what makes you feel good or gives you a sense of purpose. Broke people are a bad market. Read this paragraph over and over again until it sinks in.

In other words, you attract exactly what you project into the world— through your words, in your books, marketing materials, videos, audios or social media content.

Conversely, people who share a simple, clear transformational story that captures the heart of that customer, the benefit and the results they've experienced—and when they are really tied emotionally to that success and feel a grand great sense of purpose as a result of it—are the ones who write the best books and who also have the healthiest businesses.

The best strategy in your book is to open each chapter with a story about one person that's raw, authentic and makes a relevant point. Just like I did with this chapter when I told you the story about Lori, Steven and Richard.

If you've ever wanted to follow the best story formula that was ever created, read *Cinderella, King Arthur,* or *The Resurrection of Jesus Christ.* In all cases, they follow a model that is known in movie and script circles as the "hero's journey." (This concept was originally described and talked about by Joseph Campbell.) Historically, it's also called

If you want to watch a short (and funny) video about the "Hero's Journey" —look up "Glove and Boots Heroes Journey" on YouTube and watch it. Prepare to laugh as it's taught with puppets.

I've boiled my version of the "hero's journey" down to five simple steps that I've found to work extremely well. They are super simple. The five steps are:

1. Hope
2. Inspiration
3. Motivation
4. Transformation
5. Transcendence

Every book or product or marketing piece should do the following and in this order:

Create and connect with the reader's sense of **Hope**.

Perhaps this is the dialogue you have: *"I wish I could experience the life of a successful author. I want to be able to connect with more people and have them recognize me for the genius that I am and not have to sell myself so hard and prove myself every time I go into a meeting. I wish I could get on the TED stage, be on TV or the radio. I wish my family understand what I do and why I do it. I wish I didn't have to fight so hard to make the money I make - it seems I'm always stuck competing and reducing my rates or prices. I have trouble standing out and I don't want to brag or talk about myself even though I have 20 years of experience. Me and my message needs to get the attention I deserve so people can use my products and services."*

Sound familiar?

Next, you share stories of **Inspiration**. Ideally, share your own journey of why you do what you do or of people you've helped who got results just like you have. Connect through your pain, your vulnerabilities, your passion, your dreams and desires that your reader identifies with. Or, share a story of someone you've helped, who had a breakthrough that the reader can identify with.

"Lori spent almost five years attending conferences, buying products, hiring coaches, trying to find a solution to get and share her message with the world. Lori invested in one of Mike's training programs and decided to upgrade her experience to spend a day with Mike on his boat in the San Diego harbor for a "boatstorming" coaching session with her husband and son. She described her dream business, hopes and dreams, but didn't realize that she didn't really understand her ideal customer and upon further digging, that customer was hard to reach and didn't have the money she wanted to charge for her products and services she spent so much time making.

During that coaching session, she had a revelation and a breakthrough and finally understood why she had felt "stuck" for years, not knowing exactly what to do on her projects. She was shocked when Mike suggested that she change her focus completely and starts a new business in an industry she already had credibility, authority and expertise in and had easy access to high-quality, wealthy prospects. She was amazed when Mike told her that all she had to do is create a product offer and send it out to a few people to endorse what she was doing!"

Next, is **Motivation**. Continue on the journey. Show proof that you or your subject implemented, got results and made it through the other side.

"Lori left the "boatstorming" coaching session with a new sense of hope, clarity and vision. She realized she spent years and tens of thousands of dollars pursuing a path that wasn't going to make her happy or feel fulfilled. But more importantly, her family really understood what her goals and intentions were. Before the coaching session, they didn't really understand her BIG WHY—what was driving her to spend so much time away from her family on those trips, reading all those books and buying all those courses that seemed to take her away from them. They were so inspired after seeing Lori's

progress that Steven decided he wanted to try his hand at entrepreneurship too and turn his passion of scuba diving into a book and course. Their son Richard was also inspired and motivated and started outlining a book and business of his own while attending college."

Next, is step #4, **Transformation**. This is the moment where the "rubber meets the road" and implementation occurs. So many people complain that they're "too busy," or "too overwhelmed," that "the timing isn't right" or "other priorities are more important," that they "don't have the knowledge or resources," or that they're simply "too tired at the end of the day" to focus on what's really important in their lives.

Excuses. All excuses. Winners don't make excuses.

Chuck Yeager was the first person to break the sound barrier.

After that achievement of courage and bravery he said:

"At the moment of truth, there are either reasons or results."

Are you going to sit around and use a whole bunch of reasons (excuses) why you didn't cross the finish line or even start? Are you going to procrastinate, be weighed down by the "Yeah, Butt" monster? Will you let your message DIE inside you? Will all of your experience, wisdom and knowledge be lost without legacy? Will you wallow in your regrets?

Are you interested or are you committed in sharing your message? Reading a book about being successful won't make anyone successful without commitment and implementation.

Lori got busy. She sat down and wrote, published and promoted her book in record time. She started getting booked in the media, on television. And the more success she received, the more her confidence increased. She has clarity and focus and knows exactly what she's going to do next.

You are looking for the transformative moment, rags to riches, failure to success, sickness to health, fat to skinny, whatever the 'before' and 'after' moments are to write about.

Sometimes, it's a more nuanced and less dramatic transformation. But it needs to be a measurable change. Ideally with a situation or character that's easy to relate to. Ordinary people aren't moved by perfect people.

From a marketing perspective, on television, radio, in books and online, there are people making a lot of promises and you don't know who to trust. There's a mountain of skepticism, cynicism, broken promises and outright fabrications and lies.

What you can trust is a track record of proven results. Don't trust promises. Trust proven results. Trust irrefutable physical proof. The more proof you include in your book, the faster your reader will trust you. You can't assume the reader of your book is going to finish your book. That means every chapter should get and keep attention.

Our entire marketing strategy in our business revolves around before and after stories, pictures, videos, interviews, gathering checks, contracts and celebrating our customer's transformations. We take pictures, videos and do interviews constantly.

When you share and tell stories of transformation, people pay attention, they listen and they remember.

There's an old saying, "it's hard to be a prophet in your hometown or home." But even your family will take notice when people start walking up to them and say, "do you know how much your son/daughter/husband/wife has changed my life and how remarkable he/she really is?"

Or when a stranger walks up to you and wants you to shake your hand or have you autograph your book for them in front of a family member. That's when they take notice - you've arrived!

And look, this isn't about recognition, it's about making a genuine difference in people's lives, getting your message out to the world, being valued for who you are, not what you do.

Step #5 is **Transcendence**.

Transcendence is where community meets success. It's a business or brand culture. It's when your readers or customers talk about you and become your marketing arm, share their feelings and successes with other people online and offline. It's when your brand has a theme and continuity attached to it and your followers and fans support you and each other.

Or better yet, create a community, group or forum and your customers and clients teach and support each other or create sub-communities and sub-groups. It's family where they feel they have a home and a safe place.

Tony Robbins has a huge community of followers and fans. They all share common goals and values: passion, integration, contribution-orientation and success.

In our Publish and Profit Community, we have a private Facebook group that our customers are invited to join. The people in the community meet each other at our live events, they support each other by buying and promoting each other's books, voting on which book titles and covers they like best and answering questions. Some of them have started mastermind groups together. Others have formed business partnerships and relationships and refer business back and forth to one another - creating value.

Everybody wins. A culture and family is stronger together. For us, it lowers our support costs and increases the overall value and experience the customers get when they invest in the product.

And what's really great is all of the active, engaged members of the community reach a top 10 and most a #1 bestseller status when their books are released!

Here's a remarkable story of transformation and another example of what I consider to be a "Perfect Customer" (in addition to Lori :).

Andy was a K9 policeman for nearly 20 years. He taught dogs how to be police dogs. After being a cop for years he got himself into a couple of bad business deals that put him in debt. At some point in his career he was injured, unable to continue working and lost his job.

Andy was in over his head financially. He had an expensive lifestyle, a house, cars, a boat, and a young wife and five children. Things started to go downhill for him. His house was in foreclosure. He was on the brink of bankruptcy. His wife and he were talking about divorce. He felt extremely unsuccessful because he was struggling to not only pay his bills but also take care of his family. Anyone who's ever been that position before knows how scary and humiliating that feeling is.

At his lowest point, sheriffs that he used to work with were sent to his house to post a foreclosure notice on his home. At some point he found out about us online and managed to get a ticket to one of our live events. He had built rapport with Robin, one of our customer support representatives, who knew a little bit about his story and gave him the ticket as a gift. Andy was so broke that a friend of his loaned him money to buy gas to come to our event and while he was there, he slept in his car.

We weren't aware of Andy's challenges. However, he filled out a form to get on a "hot seat" at one of our events. That's an opportunity to be coached live in front of an audience of hundreds of people with four of us providing advice. Andy didn't share the deep trouble he was in but he did talk about something he was working on and we gave him advice for his business, his website and a book.

Andy tells a story about how he took half the "hotseat" advice we gave him and he still got results. He managed to get his feet back under him, he published his book and started booking a couple of deals as a dog trainer and consultant and made enough money to keep himself out of bankruptcy, feed his family and prevent his foreclosure. He continued participating in our community, invested in a couple of programs and instead of implementing 50% of what we told him to do, he went all in and did 100%.

Less than two years later, Andy shared a remarkable transformation with us. He had booked a $349,000 consulting deal with the country of Bahrain providing dog training services. His book enabled him to get seen on National Geographic, ABC and NBC News, The Discovery Channel and he got international clients including a French family that flew to his home in California, delivered their two dogs to him and paid him a thousand dollars per week each to train and rescue the animals.

After seeing Andy on TV, they felt he was the only person who could "fix" their dogs. It all happened because of his book!

Andy used the Publish and Profit system to write an additional book that became a bestseller in only two weeks and he recently spoke in front of a large audience at Caesars' Palace in Las Vegas and Planet Hollywood in Las Vegas.

This story doesn't capture all of the emotion that Andy felt and experienced but it does follow the five-step process quite well. Number one, Andy had hope. We gave him an opportunity to attend a live event. Someone gave him the resources and tools he needed to show up and attend despite an incredibly challenging situation. At that event, he was *inspired* by the advice he received, the community that we created and he met other people just like him who were building their futures, learning new strategies, techniques and mindset that would propel them from where they were to where they wanted to be.

Andy was deeply *motivated* by his circumstance, his family, but also by the possibility and potential that he could change his circumstance and not only get out of a difficult situation but also be free from the debt, the pain and humiliation he was experiencing.

Andy's *transformation* occurred on several levels. The first was when he implemented about half of what was recommended and he got good results. It got him out of the situation he was in but he again, was deeply motivated to not only be excellent, but to be truly extraordinary. When he decided to invest in himself again and follow the advice systems and strategies a hundred percent, his next transformation occurred and he had massive breakthroughs that have helped him earn even more money and experience an even greater transformation.

Finally, his *transcendence* came when he was able to stand up and talk at one of our events and share his whole story. Both he and I wept openly as he discussed and described what was going on with him. Much of the story I didn't even know, and I had no idea how bad his circumstance really was. But now, through his own transformation and transcendence, his story will affect other people and he's able to guide and support other people too.

I don't expect that you will have such an incredible transformation story to tell, but any time you invest in one of your clients and customers, and think of them as a potential storyteller, it will affect the way you treat them, the services and products you provide. It doesn't matter if you run a coffee shop and your goal is just to be a day maker and make someone smile or you are in the pest control industry, a financial planner, a nutritionist, a coach or a consultant. Every interaction with a client or customer can provide the five-step hero process that can also be told as a story. There is a story to be told in every interaction with every human being you ever come in contact with.

In summary, your objective and goal is to examine your business and think about your best customer you've ever had and call them your avatar. This is your ideal perfect customer: someone who pays you, implements, gets results, refers more people to you and comes back and asks for more products and services from you and willingly pays you for them. This is the person you write your book for.

CHAPTER EIGHT

Wrap Your Package with a Great Cover

> *"Really it comes down to your philosophy. Do you want to play it safe and be good or do you want to take a chance and be great?"*
>
> *Jimmy J*

Do you want the cure and the solution to selling lots of books?

It's PACKAGING.

It all begins with a great book cover that captures attention. A great book cover is easy and cheap to make.

We give things a lot more value when they're in attractive or pretty packages. *We all judge books by their covers.* We judge people, products, and services. Like it or not, the clothes we wear, cars we drive, schools we go to, people we associate with and titles we have are positioning tools that are meaningful to the people we want to do business with.

For you and your book, packaging is an easy formula to learn but most amateurs screw it up because they don't really understand they blow their chances of success by making a horrible book cover. Packaging success is a combination of a great book title, subtitle and cover. It's designed to get attention, GRAB a prospect and sell your book – while positioning you as a high-value authority.

Just do a Google search on branding, packaging and perceived value. There's a lot of science and research that supports the value of packaging not to mention the fact that it's intuitively obvious that packaging alone can multiply the perceived product by 10x or more.

Let's say you have two identical diamond rings. As a marketing test, you might write a story about how one ring was crafted by a family of multigenerational artisans from a small village in Europe. Because each ring is hand-made, the family can only make 50 per year. Each diamond is polished with a rare mineral only found in rocks brought back from the moon to give it a unique luster and sheen. Each ring is packaged in a hand-crafted display box that uses a rare type of glass made from the sands of a mountain spring lake known for its purity and clarity. The chrome like metal for the display box is mined and forged by metalsmiths and skilled glassblowers that hand craft each panel of glass for the box and numbered.

When the ring is sold at an exclusive store, it is put under bright lights, under a glass dome, surrounded by security cameras, an armed guard, a multimedia presentation that plays with classical music in the background, showing images of how that ring is hand made by each family member.

The second ring is placed loose in a matchbox and put in the "discount" section of a pawnshop.

Is it reasonable to assume the ring in the fancy "package" with a fancy presentation will fetch $10,000 - $20,000 or even $50,000 while the other identical ring would struggle to sell for $1,000?

I'm not saying you have to create an elaborate story about your book or package it in a handcrafted box. But I am saying the more "story" that someone experiences when they see your book cover, title and subtitle and feel connected to it, the more likely they will give it a chance, click on it or pick it up and buy it.

Here's a strategy I use when I need inspiration for a book title. It's based on something I call "lizard brain." I walk into a bookstore and I turn on my "lizard brain" and I look for "shiny objects" that attract my attention. I just scan and walk around. When I see a book that attracts my attention, I read the title and subtitle as if I were someone who wanted to solve the problem that the book promises. I make a list of the books that "grab" me the most. You can do this just by searching on Amazon and scrolling until something "pops" out at you.

For example, one of my favorite book covers is a book called, "Linchpin" by Seth Godin. The subtitle is, "Are you Indispensable?" The book cover is bright orange. It has a picture of a fist with a lightning bolt in it. If you walk into a bookstore and just let your eyes wonder, it's a book that stands out on the shelves. It's easy to spot, easy to find. I find that I want to reach out and grab it, and I also found that the title and subtitle is also interesting.

The first time I saw it, I bought the book. The message inspired and motivated me. I started giving it to friends, business associates and employees.

If you package your book with an amateurish cover, it looks cheap and it reflects badly on you. You can get a really, really attractive book cover made for $5-$500 on www.Fiverr.com, www.99Designs.com or www.CrowdSpring.com. It's critical that you give a designer specific direction to get great results.

One of my strategies is to search in Google images for "best book covers", find 5-10 covers that I find attractive and attention-getting, copy and paste them into a document that I share with my designers. The whole point is go out and find attractive covers that are relevant to the market and category you wish to dominate, examine the ones that are bestsellers, and model the best. Together, you can do something we call "Frankensteining" where you combine the best designs and have them made as your own.

The point of this exercise is, you don't have to reinvent the wheel and you really don't need to even know anything about design or packaging. You just copy and model the best.

Book covers that used to cost $5,000-$25,000 now can be produced for $300-$800.

CHAPTER NINE

Your Book's Title and Subtitle

"The difference between a successful person and others is not a lack of strength, not a lack of knowledge, but rather a lack of will."

Vince Lombardi

What does it take to create a real winning book title and cover that MAKES YOU MONEY?

We're going to do a little exercise in this chapter on how to write book titles and subtitles.

The exercise will help you name practically ANYTHING; not just books, but products, services, articles, videos, social media posts.

Let's begin by modeling a #1 bestselling book that's sold tens of millions of copies, *The 7 Habits of Highly Effective People,* by Stephen Covey, Ph.D.

Here is the secret to a great book title: just make spaces and keep the formula.

Here is what I mean by this:

The 7 Secrets of Highly Effective People becomes...

The _____(Blank) *Secrets of Highly Effective* _____(Blank).

Now let's create a new title for your business. Let's say you're in the mortgage business. Here are a few titles for you if your target audience is mortgage brokers:

The 10 Secrets of Highly Effective Mortgage Brokers

or

The 3 Secret Sentences to Closing More Mortgage Deals

or

The 7 Secrets of Highly Engaging Mortgage Brokers

Here's another example:

Simply take a successful book title and adapt it to your niche. So, you could take the book: *Think and Grow Rich* by Napoleon Hill. Our customer Lori Barr used this formula to create her #1 bestselling book, *Think and Grow Well.* Of course, Lori is a doctor, so this worked perfectly for her. Maybe you're not a doctor; but if you're in fitness, you could use:

Lift and Grow Strong

or

Run and Grow Fast

or

Eat and Grow Slim

Let me share some examples of great book covers, titles and subtitles some of our customers did in just a few minutes. We include professionally-designed done-for-you book covers and 3D images with our training system.

Here's Karol Clark's new book, *Build the Weight Loss Practice of Your Dreams: Your Blueprint for a Successful Weight Loss Practice that Creates a Healthy Bottom Line.* Karol is connecting with her ideal audience by selling a benefit... and she also used a clever double meaning when she shows them how they can have a "healthy" bottom line.

Here's a fun one from 40-year-veteran pest exterminator Dale Bell. After just a few minutes with the "Million Dollar Book Titles and Covers" exercise, he came up with:

Things That Crawl in the Night: Life Without Bugs

I don't know about you, but I think this book would also make an AWESOME interview on NPR, a national or local radio program, a podcast, video series or on flyers to hand out at a local event. It will definitely differentiate him from other exterminators and make him and his business more approachable and show he has a sense of humor. It's fun, memorable and clear. Not bad for a few minutes of brainstorming, right?

This last example should answer the question I get asked all the time, "Will this work in my business?" The answer is YES. If it can work for bugs and ants and rats, it can work for you, human. This will work for you in any niche, any business, on any topic, anywhere in the world.

If you're interested in writing faith-based, spiritual or religious books, you'll enjoy this example:

Please God and Prosper: Getting to Abundance Without Losing Your Soul, by Dr. Emma Jean Thompson. It was patterned after the perennial *New York Times* #1 bestseller, *How to Win Friends and Influence People.* She also brilliantly answers one key objection about abundance and money... which is people feeling like they will lose their soul if they get it. Well done, Emma!

I love this one:

50 Shades of Wealth: How to Master and Dominate Your Financial Future by Thomas Watts; patterned, of course, after the blockbuster book series, *50 Shades of Gray.* He even cleverly embedded the words "Master" and "Dominate." This example would fly off the shelves and is practically guaranteed to get media interviews and attention. It can also be easily turned into a podcast; series of YouTube videos; articles; social media posts; heck, even live events and products. It's absolutely CATCHY - and will appeal to both men and women.

As of the time I'm writing this to you, it's also very timely. If your goal isn't to write a book that has a long shelf life, you can take advantage of media, movies, celebrity and current events. One of our customers wrote a book about Ebola when it was a huge scare and being covered in the national media.

And here's another winner that is directly targeted towards the printing industry:

Print Money: Strategies to Turn Your Printing Business into a Money Making Machine Without Resorting to Counterfeiting by Ian Bosler. This is super catchy and really fun and goes to show that this strategy will work in any industry—even in brick and mortar businesses.

Here's a secret that the big publishers and their attorneys don't want you to know: a book title can't be copyrighted. This means you can pattern or model it, without any restrictions, unless it is TRADEMARKED. Now, for the record, I'm not an attorney. I'm not giving you legal advice; so don't do anything dumb or without professional legal guidance, okay?

Again… the possibilities are endless. You just need to find a book title you like and modify it to fit your market and theme.

In our system, we include some great resources to make this process even easier including software that writes your book titles for you.

Now… here is a massive breakthrough secret to getting your book to sell and become a bestseller: Amazon let's you publish a book before it is written!

All you have to do is upload a cover, a description and Amazon lists it for pre-order sale. You can test out your ideas before you've written anything. Amazon takes orders, collects money and starts charting your sales; and you can become a bestseller in less than a week… and you don't even have to be done with your book! How cool is that?

Do you think you would get a book done if it was ALREADY a bestseller and you had a hard deadline to hit?

Yes! And if the book doesn't pick up steam and get orders as soon as you publish it you can remove the book a few hours later and try out a different idea. You can literally test out several book ideas at once and only finish the real winners!

Andy Falco used our process and pre-published his next book, *Dog Training for Fun and Profit: Earn Big Profits while Creating a Loving and Respectful Relationship between Humans and their Dogs*. He posted it in our private, members-only community, hit #1 in a day and got a speaking engagement for 800 people at Caesar's Palace!

By now, that should put away any fears you might have if you've been asking disempowering questions like:

"I don't have time to write a book."

"WHAT WILL I PUT IN MY BOOK?"

"I'm not a writer! Who am I anyway?"

"Who's going to listen to me?"

"WHO WILL BUY IT?"

"WHO WILL CARE?"

The fact is, everyone who's ever become anyone has probably felt that same way when they started out... but they eventually received the guidance and coaching they needed or found a formula or system that worked for them. In the past, that could take months or years to learn; and it often took 1.5 to 3 years to write and get published the "old way."

"How can I wrap my book around my business or my business around my book?" It's really very easy...

To wrap a book around your business that already exists, use a proven system, tell stories and answer questions. You're already doing whatever will go into your books. If you're not an expert or don't know the answers, ask or interview other experts and people who have already done it themselves; that's part of a proven step-by-step process and coaching, and it will collapse what used to take years into weeks or even days.

You have a perfect book title formula tool in your pocket right now if you have the Amazon app on your smartphone. Just search for book topics and look for formulas can model and reuse. You don't have to think that hard. You don't have to reinvent the wheel, just be careful to not be vague or clever.

And you don't have to be perfect either. You can always change the title, subtitle and your book cover later. Just upload a new title and cover and it'll be live in a few hours on Amazon! It just has to be good enough. *Perfection is the enemy of done.*

This is NOT an excuse to produce a bad book filled with spelling, grammatical errors or inaccuracies. There's a great quote that I believe is from Stephen Spielberg – "no film is ever completed, it is only abandoned." I've seen that quote attributed to an author – "no book is ever completed, only abandoned."

At some point, you've just got to let it go, put it online, sell it and reap the rewards. Your book doesn't do anyone, especially you any good if it sits on your hard drive for months or years.

GET FEEDBACK ON YOUR BOOK TITLE

Is it catchy enough? Will it capture your potential buyer's attention? Get feedback from me and fellow authors on what title is likely to generate more sales and more with the Publish and Profit system:

Visit www.PublishAndProfit.com/BookBonus
or text your email address to (858) 707-7417

CHAPTER TEN

Your Content - Connect with Your Reader

"Success is...knowing your purpose in life, growing to reach your maximum potential, and sowing seeds that benefit others."

John C. Maxwell

The next step is content. It might seem strange that this is the last segment of the "Prepare" step. Most people make a big mistake and think the content is where they should begin. Until you've identified <u>why</u> you're writing your book, <u>who</u> you writing it for, <u>what</u> your cover, your title and subtitle are, focusing on content is a waste of time because you'll possibly write a book nobody will buy or read.

Here's how to quickly create the best content that will get you the most results and be super easy to make at the same time. It's the fastest, quickest, and most effective way to become an instant expert or "extract" content and knowledge from another expert.

It's called "The 10x10 Formula."

I've taught this process to hundreds of thousands of people over the past decade and it works for books, online videos, podcasts, blog content, articles and even getting media attention.

The formula is based on a simple premise. If you are in business or work for someone who does, you get asked the same questions over and over about your products, services, know-how, expertise, wisdom, passions or life experience.

If you just sat down and wrote down all the questions you get asked all the time, recorded those answers in your smartphone and transcribed them, you'd have a book of the majority of your knowledge in less than a day.

If you packaged this information and sold it, you'd probably make money and help a lot of people at the same time, anytime, anywhere and in multiple countries or languages.

Here's the formula that you can use to unlock years or decades of your expertise, genius, wisdom, knowledge and value:

1. Set a timer for three minutes
2. Sit down with a piece of paper.
3. Draw a line down the middle of the page.
4. On the left, write "FAQs" - these are "Frequently Asked Questions."
5. On the right, write "SAQs" - these are "Should Ask Questions."

FAQs are questions people might ask you when they want to learn more about your area of knowledge or expertise, NOT your products or services.

The goal of the FAQs is to educate without selling. Talk about your prospects, not you. Give them answers to their questions, but do not hit them with a sales pitch. When you do it this way, you create engagement, connection and desire.

This also works for when you do interviews because it builds your brand by associating yourself with other experts or celebrities. It's been the #1 way I've managed to connect and partner with my celebrity clients including Tony Robbins, John Assaraf, Brian Tracy, Paul Abdul and JJ Virgin.

The SAQs or Should Ask Questions are the questions you WISH people would ask you BECAUSE IT IS THE STUFF THAT PEOPLE DON'T KNOW THAT THEY DON'T KNOW... It's nuanced knowledge.

These are the things you may have spent 5, 10, or even 30+ years studying and refining to figure out. It's your wisdom. This knowledge has come to you after thousands of hours of hard work, practice, making mistakes, and working in the trenches.

When you've studied your craft for that long, you often learn a lot of myths that other people believe - and that's why SAQs can make great mythbusters. SAQs are trust-builders and differentiators. Your answers are uniquely yours – and they help you stand out in a crowd.

It's important to point out that the BEST FAQs and SAQs are demonstrations or stories - you show someone a "before and after" and show them how to get results step-by-step without any fluff.

The biggest difference between FAQs and SAQs is that an FAQ is generally what people search for online. These are like little "money magnets" that establish the fact that you're a knowledgeable resource.

Of course money magnets are important, but the SAQs are what MAKE YOU THE EXPERT and grow your value. When people hear your response to an SAQ, they will be captivated by your knowledge, expertise, passion, know-how and wisdom.

They'll be glued to your every word and realize that they couldn't possibly do whatever you offer on their own, and they wouldn't want to buy anything else or a competitive product. They'll know YOU'RE the answer to their problem or challenge. You're automatically positioned as a leader and expert - and all humans are attracted to smart leaders they relate and feel connected to.

To gain this positioning in your target audience's mind, all you have to do is answer some questions. How easy is that?

Next, you record your answers to these questions simply into your smartphone, tablet, computer, video or audio recorder.

Transcribe them.

And you'll soon have great content for a book.

In my experience, about 20 questions can be answered in 3-6 hours and equates into a 100-120 page book with a bit of editing.

Let me prove to you how much wisdom, knowledge and genius is in your head right now.

Set a timer for 3 minutes.

As fast as you can, write down as many FAQs and SAQs as you can before the timer runs out.

In my experience, most people come up with 5-10.

So if you come up with 5, that means you could come up with 100 in an hour.

If you wrote down 10, that's 200 questions in an hour.

Most people can write down 200 different questions they get asked all the time in an hour or so.

Using this simple model, it might seem hard to believe, but that's about 3-5 books worth of content that's already inside you!

This same model can be used to create videos, podcasts, articles or interviews. It's a complete "content map" you can use for years.

A 10x10 Example - an Interview

Here's a 10x10 project I made with the author, Tim Ferriss.

I invited him to my studio in San Diego to promote his book *The Four Hour Body*. I lost 17 pounds and four inches off my waist in 30 days using his system, so I wanted to share my results with the world.

In this instance, I made interview videos with him but I could have turned all of them into book chapters and put it on Amazon and sold it as a book.

I read his book and came up with a list of 10x10 questions I thought people would want to know (FAQs) and should know (SAQs) and interviewed him over a period of a couple of hours in my studio. But I could have just as easily interviewed him with Skype, Google Hangouts or on the phone

Here's an example of some of the top 10 FAQs (Frequently Asked Questions):

1. What is *The Four Hour Body*, who is it for and what inspired you to create it?
2. How does *The Four Hour Body* work and how can people take advantage of it?
3. What are 3 roadblocks or objections that would prevent skeptics from giving *The Four Hour Body* a fair try?
4. What are the biggest MYTHS about weight loss you can share?

At the end of each video, we added a "Call to Action" that drove people directly to the www.FourHourBodyBook.com web site.

Next, I came up with the top ten Should Ask Questions and did the same as above.

Here's an example of some of the SAQs (Should Ask Questions):

1. What's ONE question that you haven't been asked but always wanted to answer from the moment you wrote *The Four Hour Body?*
2. What should everyone know about life extension that they don't ask about?
3. What's the most important tip you can pass along to someone who's trying to figure out "where to begin"?
4. You have a whole chapter devoted to increasing (in your case, tripling) testosterone. Why is this important and what can men do about it?

And when I finished these, I recorded a special "behind the scenes bonus video" that we gave away to anyone who bought the book. I called it "Success Leaves Clues."

Here's an example of some questions that might get your "10x10" juices flowing. These are questions anyone can answer, but your answers are going to be completely unique in comparison to the next person answering them. And because you're unique, your answers will immediately prove that you're an expert in your field:

1. What personal attributes, traits, or qualities have most contributed to your success? How did you develop these qualities?
2. Can you give specific examples of when these traits have played a role in your path towards success?
3. What were some of the major adversities and trials that you had to overcome to achieve your goals?
4. What kept you going despite these obstacles? Why didn't you give up?
5. Who motivated or inspired you when you were younger or began your journey to where you are today?

That's it! A start-to-finish example of how the 10x10 formula works. I've helped thousands of small business owners, entrepreneurs, authors, experts, speakers and consultants in virtually every business imaginable do this.

This strategy works like crazy because you're creating really good content that the search engines and people love video AND books!

It naturally develops rapport and an emotional connection and bond that is only better with direct one-on-one touch.

If you want to give your book content an extra boost of readability and interest, begin every chapter with a short story that illustrates what you're about to teach. The human brain is more attracted to stories than it is to facts. Stories are easier to remember and relate to when those facts are associated with people and emotions.

Stories create a bond with a non-buyer who recognizes and feels your sense of mission, your heart and big why. It's a great way to get content out of your head and onto a page and it's also extremely effective if you want to write a book with experts and benefit from an association with celebrity or brand.

If you don't have time or stories for every chapter, don't let that stop you from finishing your book. Like the cover, you can always add more content to your book and republish in a couple of hours. It will take more thought and time but it will result in a much better content and it will create a deeper bond and connection with your reader and your audience.

Once you've finished your content and storytelling, your book can be repurposed into an audio book, podcast, videos, social media content or even training modules or products.

CONTENT CREATION IDEAS

Having trouble getting your creative juices flowing? Get new content ideas and fill-in-the-blank templates that make telling your story easier than ever.

Visit www.PublishAndProfit.com/BookBonus
or text your email address to (858) 707-7417

CHAPTER ELEVEN

Step #2–Perform

"If you genuinely want something, don't wait for it – teach yourself to be impatient."

Gurbaksh Chahal

When I wrote my very first book, I had less than an hour of strength every day while being treated for cancer at the Duke Medical Cancer Center. I was getting daily doses of radiation and oral chemotherapy that made me feel like I was a crippled 90-year-old man. Every day I woke up in a pile of my hair in my pillow that fell out of my head the night before. I was weak and tired. I was absolutely miserable and spent most of my day either in the fetal position lying in bed or in the bathroom.

Despite that circumstance, I was driven by a sense of mission and urgency. Like anyone who's ever been taken down by a horrible disease, I was the guy who said, "it'll never happen to me" but when it did, I felt the sense of loss and fear that I might leave the planet without sharing my knowledge, wisdom and message. For the first time in my life, at age 46, I understood the concept of legacy. And I also feared for my wife and son. I needed to find a way to communicate, but also to provide a means of income in the event I died.

A book seemed like an appropriate way to do that.

So in less than an hour a day, I laid in bed and spoke each chapter of my book into my iPhone and sent the recordings to be transcribed and edited by someone else.

I answered the most common frequently asked questions I got from people who responded to a survey about marketing, list-building, growing their business, overwhelm, procrastination, building authority, credibility, getting traffic, making content and more. Over 800 people shared what they wanted to learn from me...and then I just answered questions!

My prescription to their "disease" and challenges was to write a book. Up until that point I had self-published a few things, dabbled and had created and produced lots of manuals and products, but I had never written a book myself

But what uniquely qualified me to write books was the fact that I had been consulting and coaching authors, experts, speakers, consultants, coaches, entrepreneurs and small business owners on book marketing for years. My wife is a twice-published author. I had also been trained by a multiple bestselling author, Arielle Ford, who was well-known as a great publicist and had represented 11 NY Times #1 Bestselling Authors including Deepak Chopra, Wayne Dyer, Marianne Williamson, Don Miguel Ruiz, Dr. Dean Ornish, Debbie Ford, Louise Hay (of Hay House), Jack Canfield, Mark Victor Hansen and Neale Donald Walsch.

This was back when becoming a bestseller wasn't easily "rigged" or "gamed" with online gimmicks. Authors went on book tours that lasted for months, signing books at bookstores, speaking, presenting and doing hundreds of radio and TV shows.

I had created and produced a product about publishing; publicity, promotion and building platforms that had been selling for nearly 10 years. I knew the complexities of writing, publishing and promoting books.

So, driven by fear of death and lack of legacy, I thought I'd teach what I knew and create a "How To" book too.

So, armed with my trusty iPhone, an hour of strength a day and a clear vision and list of questions to answer, I started recording. From the moment I decided to write the book, it was written, published, promoted and became a #1 bestseller in 28 days – while going through cancer treatment!

The most effective way to connect with your audience is to answer questions chapter by chapter in your book and begin with the story first. It humanizes you and the subject matter, and it creates a memorable conversation in the reader's mind that is not only emotionally charged but it is much easier to remember.

Just look at what you read - this is a business book and I opened this chapter with a very vulnerable, emotionally charged story that is relevant and I hope, memorable. You gained an insight into me that I hope you relate to and connect with because perhaps, you share the same fears that I have.

Even if your goal is to write a business book, this strategy applies. When you think about the books that you really like, that you learn the most from, and are the most memorable, I'm guessing you'll find that the best incorporate a story that follows the hero's arc with a definite beginning, middle, and end with some kind of struggle and resolve at the end.

Before I write a book, I sit down with three to five of my favorite books and I skim and read a few chapters. I pay very close attention to the structure and the tone of the conversation in each of them. I spend time in a space of *feeling*, not thinking.

For example, Darren Hardy, publisher of *Success* magazine, is one of my favorite authors and he's also a good friend. He's extremely passionate and smart. He has a very pragmatic way of teaching and talking, both in person and in his books. Another author that I find particularly engaging and interesting is Tim Ferriss. Tim's content and his perspective on the world is always useful to me. I really resonate with his books, blog and podcast.

Pay close attention to what works best for you and model it. And when and while you're writing, it is much easier to create a structure that is easy to follow when it and your emotional state is fresh in your mind.

Enhance your book with pictures, proof, examples, and stats. It's super easy to find supplemental content, research, data and relevant information with a simple Google search. You can easily hire someone on a design site like Fiverr, eLance, Freelancer, 99Designs or CrowdSpring to take your data and turn it into infographics or illustrations for $5-$25 in a couple days.

If you speak or perform on stage or like to teach or sell with Keynote or PowerPoint, then perform your content and record it as if you are presenting or performing in front of a live audience. It makes the content dynamic, interesting, very conversational, and is easy to transcribe and edit.

It's my opinion that business books that are designed to capture leads and grow a business should focus on the "what" and not the "how." The *how* is what you sell in your programs and products. And just to be transparent and give you full disclosure, we teach you the "how" of publishing in our *Publish and Profit* product and include tools, resources, templates, and step-by-step instructions so that you can write a good book in days or weeks instead of months or years.

That is exactly what this book is – there's plenty of "how to" in this book, but I'm really giving you a lot of reasons why you should write, publish, promote and become a bestseller. Giving you all the how-to details is way beyond the scope and capability of what can be taught in a book. My step-by-step course includes video training, templates, tools and resources that aren't realistically or reasonably possible to deliver in this book. The important thing for you to realize is I practice what I preach – and it works!

An effective business book not only gets the reader interested in what you have to share by understanding the "what," but it also intrigues them enough with the "how" so that the book is a lead generator and drives *qualified* traffic to your business. By design, it drives people to your website for a sample of your program or product and opportunity to speak with a salesperson or consultant, a place to get a diagnostic tool, or some sort of training audios or videos to engage and deepen the relationship further.

The equipment and gear that we recommend for performing your book is probably in your pocket right now. I'm a big fan of using an iPhone and simply plug a lavalier microphone directly into it. Moments from now, you can be talking, presenting, and performing the content for your book practically anywhere you go - even in your car. Of course, you can use any laptop or desktop computer too. The microphones that I recommend and use personally are Blue Microphones, and the two models I frequently use are the Nessie and the Yeti, just search for "Blue Nessie" or "Blue YETI" on Amazon for less than $100.

One of the services I use is Rev.com – with it, you can record audio on an App, press a button and send it to be transcribed. Within a couple of hours you receive a full transcription, formatted in a Microsoft Word or text file. It costs $1 per recorded minute.

I "wrote" my first book while I had cancer with an iPhone, and since we've refined this process even further, we've had hundreds of clients writing, publishing, promoting, and becoming bestselling authors using the same model from every walk of life, everywhere in the world even though they don't consider themselves to be writers.

I wrote two of my books driving in my car – it takes about 15 minutes to travel from my house to the studio so I would brainstorm some ideas while I ate breakfast in the morning and dictate the answers on each ride. In less than two weeks I had the core content for an entire book!

Most people I speak to believe that in order to write a book you've got a lock yourself up in a cabin like Henry David Thoreau and drop out of society for months or years without any interruptions. That just isn't true.

In my experience, you can create all the content you need for a 120 to 140-page book in about a day once you go through the preparation process. And if you aren't an expert or an authority or don't feel you are one, but want to help someone you know or love to write a book, you can sit down with them and interview them by asking them ten frequently asked questions, ten should ask questions, and ideally ask them to preface the answer to each question with a brief success story about each one. That will make the book significantly more compelling, and a lot of experts actually find that to be relatively easy to do if they're asked the question and they are prepped properly.

If you're struggling trying to determine good questions to ask, search for questions that are frequently asked on whatever that subject matter is in Google or look through the table of contents of the most popular books on whatever topic you're focusing on by clicking on the "Look Inside" link on any book on Amazon.

If you have a following on social media or have a list, send out a survey to them with an offer to get a copy of your new book for free when it's released.

CHAPTER TWELVE

Step #3–Publish

"If you have a dream, don't just sit there. Gather courage to believe that you can succeed and leave no stone unturned to make it a reality."

Roopleen

Now that you've performed your content and transcribed your content into a book format (more or less), your goal is to make sure your content is published everywhere so you can be seen, and ideally, heard and read, listened to and watched on any device anywhere, anytime.

Whoa!

That doesn't make sense.

I thought we're talking about books, right?

Well, we are and we aren't.

You can publish your content so it can be seen, heard, read, listened to, viewed and watched on any device anywhere, anytime, and on as many channels as possible, which would include billions of tablets—iPads, Kindles and Android devices. There are currently nearly four billion smartphones in use worldwide. There are approximately three billion internet-connected desktop and laptop computers, and if you think a little bit outside the box, your book content could be converted into video podcasts or a documentary so your content can be watched on a television.

Your objective for your book should be to be accessible to an audience of billions, and once you've created your book, it is relatively easy to convert your book content into derivative content including an audio book, videos, podcasts, documentary shows, articles in social media content, infographics and content that can be used in traditional media like radio, television and print. You can also actually create your book during the performance process, and make a book from other content creation strategies. The bottom line is once you've determined what your content is, your next goal is to publish it in as many formats and on as many channels as possible.

Here are some of the channels you can take advantage of to distribute your content: On Amazon, you can publish on both Kindle format as well as paperback with their CreateSpace program (which requires absolutely no cost or expense on your behalf). One of the best things about Amazon is they not only allow you to publish your electronic book and your physical book for free, they pay you up to 70% sales commissions, and market and promote your books for you.

Amazon also gives you a great "Author Page" that ranks high in search engines and allows you to upload pictures, videos, scheduled events, post your bio and links to all of your books too. Amazon is in effect, endorsing you!

For an example of what an Amazon author page looks like, you can see my Amazon author page at www.Amazon.com/author/mikekoenigs.

If you want your book to be distributed through other channels, one of our favorite services is BookBaby. BookBaby will distribute your book just about everywhere else including Apple iBooks and the Apple Store on Kobo, Gardner's Book, eCentral, Flipkart, Ciando, Barnes and Noble, Baker & Taylor, Scribd, and Oyster. Amazon's CreateSpace service will also allow you to list your book in the Ingram catalog -- one of the largest book distributors in the world! That will make your book accessible and available to major retailers worldwide.

Another very important channel that we recommend is to record an audio version of your book, and distribute it through Amazon's ACX program. This will make your book content available as an audiobook on Amazon Audible and Apple iTunes stores. Again, you'll get paid a substantial royalty, and they also have some fantastic programs that connect you with voiceover talent who will read your book and do all of the production work for you. Just like the rest of Amazon's publishing services, distribution as an audiobook is 100% free and has no risk whatsoever.

Getting into the step-by-step details about how to format and upload your book is way beyond the scope of this book. However, formatting your content for publishing is very easy. For Kindle and the electronic formats, you simply upload your book in a Microsoft Word format.

For your paperback book, you will want to have someone layout your content professionally and give you a PDF file, or you can do it yourself by buying a template for Microsoft Word, or using software for a PC or Mac called Scrivener. Scrivener outputs every known publishing format available.

Amazon's Createspace has rules and guidelines for the technical side of publishing. However, writing and publishing is 10% technology and 90% psychology. Finding people who know how to DO the tech stuff is easy and affordable.

However, _Promotion_ and _Profit_ is what everyone needs to learn in order to be successful. Knowing how to market and promote your book in every distribution channel is what will give you a huge competitive edge in every aspect of your life and help you reap the rewards of what writing a book can do for you.

Otherwise, it's wasted energy.

Here's where I'll insert a "shameless plug" for our "Publish and Profit" course. It's a step-by-step course that includes all the templates, tools, training, how-to videos and resources you need to write, publish, promote and sell your book and over a dozen ways to profit from it.

We also have a "Done With You" service if you want to work with a professional certified coach who can guide you through the book preparation, writing, publishing, promotion and profit process step-by-step and do the heavy lifting and techie stuff for you.

OK, that's enough of a sales pitch! Please don't confuse this with anything other than massive enthusiasm for a product I really believe in. It represents my legacy and I really feel strongly that as creators and business people, we have a right and a responsibility to help people get results. It's an injustice to them (and you) if you don't give people a chance to go to the next step.

PUBLISHING TIPS AND INSPIRATION

Perhaps you know your book's purpose and have written part of it, now what? The process of actually just starting or publishing your book is often the most daunting and where a lot of people give up.

Learn how you can get step-by-step instructions for getting your book online and in stores, by heading to
www.PublishAndProfit.com/BookBonus
or text your email address to (858) 707-7417

CHAPTER THIRTEEN

Step #4—Promote

"The question isn't who is going to let me;
it's who is going to stop me."

Ayn Rand

Now we're getting to the fun stuff - promotion! Once you prepared and figured out who you're speaking to; you've uncovered your "Big Why;" you figured out how to wrap your package with a beautiful cover (that didn't cost you a lot of money); created your title and subtitle; performed your content with compelling, interesting stories; and you published your content in as many formats as possible, now you need to launch your book and become the bestselling author that you know that you are.

Here's the good news.

Because Amazon and potentially half a dozen other services will be promoting your book, it's fairly easy to become a top 10 bestseller, and in many cases, a #1 best-selling author in a specific category without having to sell an enormous number of books. That is, as long as you understand how the system works.

In our Publish and Profit course, we've reverse-engineered Amazon's algorithms to accurately figure out how many books you need to sell in a day to become a #1 category bestseller. Generally speaking, you only need to sell between 40-200 in a single day to achieve that status and I've hit #1 in the marketing category with as few as 400 sales in a single day. Once you understand how to drive traffic to your page and put together a promotion, this is achievable for just about anyone.

Just as a point of contrast, it generally takes approximately 7,500-12,000 sales per week to reach a NY Times #1 Bestseller status. The variation is affected by who else is on the charts during that time – so if you're unlucky enough to launch your book the same week that someone famous does, it's harder than heck to reach the top rung.

The good news is that if you don't reach #1 the first time on Amazon's charts, you can always relaunch again later. With the NY Times, if you don't make it in the first two weeks, you never get a second chance.

Remember, this isn't all about just selling books; it's about really making certain that your book has maximum impact, is read, and drives highly qualified traffic and leads back to your business marketing funnel.

If your goal is to just share your message and help people and you don't care about making money or driving business back to you, that's ok, too. You still want to distribute your book and derivative content to as many people and marketing channels as possible.

There are a couple of critical elements to make this work. First, you need to make certain that every chapter in your book includes a call to action that provides a compelling reason to learn more about you, your products and your services, and gives them a reason to call a phone number, text their contact information to you, or visit a website. But in order for that to happen, of course, you need to sell books.

The two primary things you need in place are (1) a book selling website, and (2) a high quality mechanism to capture leads as many ways as possible. There are several tools that we have built inside our software system, Instant Customer, to automate this process and I'll describe them to you now.

The first is something we call the **Instant Publishing Machine.** This is a simple, one-page website that sells your book for you:

- It has an Amazon Buy Button on it, or buttons to purchase your book from as many different places or locations as possible.
- There's usually a video from you that starts playing when the webpage loads up that tells you what the book is about, who it's for, and why you want to buy it.

- It includes a description of some bonuses that your audience will receive when they purchase the book and forward you the receipt.
- And, below a picture of the book, there is generally a biography and a picture of the author, and of course, the email address that your audience will use to forward the receipt after they purchase your book.

You can see what a Publishing Machine looks like at www.PublishAndProfitBook.com.

There's a really important reason why you need a site like this. Amazon does not share book buyers with you. No publisher gives you buyer information of your books because the resellers don't give it to them. They know how valuable buyer information is – so if you want to build a list, you've got to figure out how to do it yourself.

That's one of the biggest reasons why you need a book selling website.

Aside from selling your book, this is the first step in building a relationship with your reader and an opportunity to start a sales cycle with them too. But how are you going to do that if Amazon isn't giving you a list of all the buyers of your books?

To get around the fact that Amazon doesn't give you the buyer information, when the customer presses the "Buy Now" button and buys your book, they're asked to forward the receipt to a special email address in exchange for receiving some great bonus gifts, videos or updates.

If your customer buys a physical copy of the book, the receipt includes the phone number and physical mailing address of the buyer too. This is an incredibly valuable resource for you, because if you have the buyer's name, email address, physical address, and phone number, you can follow up and build a significant relationship that can easily turn into a high-paying customer!

To be clear, you've been given the "keys to the kingdom" when you use this specific formula:

1. Someone buys your book - a paying customer
2. They forward their receipt to a specific address
3. You have their name

4. Their email address
5. And possibly their phone number (probably a mobile phone) and most likely, their home address if they ordered your physical book

The #1 rule of marketing is if you have someone who is INTERESTED in your topic, a RECENT BUYER and you have their DIRECT CONTACT INFORMATION, you can bring a $0.99 or $9.99 buyer straight into a $100, $500, $5,000 or even $50,000 purchase decision if you have the right "sales funnel" for a valuable product in place.

That's tool #1 every published author needs, an **Instant Publishing Machine** for selling your books and building a list of buyers.

Every author needs Tool #2, a **Crowd Grabber** which is a lead capture system. That's a mobile-responsive website that can capture a name and email address and looks and behaves properly on computers, tablets, phones or whatever gadgets are coming out next.

This is an example of a Crowd Grabber lead capture page that you can see at www.PublishAndProfit.com/BookBonus:

More than 60% of all web traffic comes from mobile phones. What if you're making a presentation on a stage, at a trade show, doing a radio or TV interview? What if someone watches your video on YouTube from his or her mobile phone? How can you capture leads from people who don't have their computer handy?

For that, you want to be able to capture leads from other sources like a mobile phone number and maybe a short code, a QR code or voice call. If you're at a live event or trade show, you'd also want a flyer with multiple ways to capture leads and a slide to insert into a Keynote or PowerPoint presentation that you can hand out on a trade show floor, at an event or speaking engagement.

The key to earning more and having more impact is to be constantly build a database of prospects so you can communicate with them when your book is launched, a new product is released, when you are doing a live event or want to promote or market a partner or vendor.

Here's an example of a "Crowd Grabber" flyer we use at events, trade shows and live presentations.

This flyer design can be blown up and turned into a sign at a trade show, handed out at events, converted into an advertisement for a newspaper or magazine, put on a table stand in a restaurant, the applications are endless. Every business should be capturing leads constantly. This simple tool has been responsible for making our clients tens, hundreds of thousands, even millions of dollars!

Over the past few years, we've built "**Crowd Grabber**" *marketing machines* that combine all of these features and functions in one place that are being used by celebrities and *New York Times* best-selling authors including Jack

Canfield, JJ Virgin, Darren Hardy from *Success* magazine, Daniel Amen, and even Academy Award-winning actor, Richard Dreyfuss to sell their books, capture leads, build their databases and make millions of dollars worth of their products, services, training, live events...because they understand the massive value of list-building.

Here's an example of a "Crowd Grabber" slide that we insert into a Keynote or PowerPoint presentation when we speak on stage, on webcasts, webinars or any time you can tell an audience to user their mobile phones to get more information:

FREE Publish and Profit Book and Video Training Bonuses

Get your free book and bonuses **INSTANTLY**!
Text your email address to
(858) 707-7417

A 5-Step System for Attracting
***PAYING* Coaching and Consulting Clients, Traffic and Leads, Product Sales and Speaking Engagements**

Imagine you're presenting in front of an audience and you want to capture the email addresses of everyone in the room. You can say something like this:

"I see you're busy taking notes. Would you like a copy of my presentation and my new book? This way you can just pay close attention to what I'm sharing with you and we can have a great connection..." Then you show this slide and inform the audience that they should text their email address to the phone number on the screen and they'll receive a copy of the presentation and your book!"

My friend Jack Canfield uses the Crowd Grabber - here's what he says:

"Hi, I'm Jack Canfield, the co-creator of "Chicken Soup for the Soul" series, co-author of "The Success Principles," and featured teacher in the movie "The Secret."

I probably do a hundred talks a year to hundreds of thousands of people in my audiences. I've sold a half a billion books. That's 500 million books, and one of the big challenges in this business we're all in, whether we're selling information or expertise, is we want to keep track of our fans, the people that listen to us, that hear us, so we have a database that we can communicate with afterwards.

And you know, one of the great tools that will help you do that: my friend Mike Koenigs has created is something called the Crowd Grabber. Now I only learned about this a couple months ago, but it has radically changed the data capture, in terms of me being able to communicate with the people that I speak to.

I recently spoke to 4,000 people at a multi-level marketing company, and normally, in the old way, where I'd have people give me a business card or fill out a form, I might capture 20% of the audience's names, addresses, emails, and so forth.

With the Crowd Grabber, I was able to use a texting system where people just text their email address right there in the moment from their mobile phone. Right there in the middle of my speech and we got 3,400 names. That's the largest capture rate I've ever had in my career and we were able to instantly send them something that was really valuable to make sure they were getting something of instant value from us.

Now we have converted many of those people into our Coaching Program, into our Summer Training, and people on our mailing list getting our E-zine that we'll have as customers for years and years to come. So, if you want to take your data capture and work with people you want to stay in touch with, I want to encourage you to work with Mike Koenigs.

You can go to his website and learn about it. And I want to strongly encourage you to take this seriously. This is a quantum leap. Just like the internet took us to a whole new level, I promise you these two tools will take you and your business to a whole new level."

(you can watch a video version of this testimonial at: http://0s4.com/r/JACKC)

This in my opinion is the single most powerful way to build an incredibly valuable, highly responsive, highly motivated list in minutes. If you take some time to build rapport and connection after you speak with a high-quality group, you can potentially turn 100 people who paid $1,000 or more to be in the room into tens or hundreds of thousands of dollars in revenue in a matter of days or weeks.

With the *Crowd Grabber Marketing Machine*, you can build a mobile-responsive website, flyer and slide in a matter of minutes that can capture leads from any device, whether it is a computer, mobile phone, or tablet, and that same campaign allows you to capture leads with a mobile phone number, a short code, a QR code, and a voice call. All of this is integrated in such a way that leads can be captured from inside your book, online through social media at live events of trade shows, in calls or in the media. It is incredibly flexible and simple to use, and very, very effective.

Those tools are all included in our Publish and Profit system - and when you visit the link below or text your email address to the phone number listed on this page, you will be able to try them out and see for yourself how they work. They're live demos!

BTW - the phone number that we use in this book is US-based. If you're located in a different country, our mobile text system supports dozens of different countries including Australia, Austria, Belgium, Canada, Estonia, Finland, Hong Kong, Ireland, Lithuania, Norway, Poland, Spain, Sweden, Switzerland, United Kingdom and of course the United States.

Here's the golden rule of list-building and marketing: *The more ways you capture leads, the more devices you support, the more channels you follow up on, the more leads and attention you'll get and you'll make more sales.*

That's Tool #2, The **Crowd Grabber**. It's all about building a list.

Tool #3 every author and business owner needs **distribution**. You want to make sure that your book is seen and read about in as many places as possible online.

Ideally, you want to share links to your book, graphics that you want distributed all over the internet, videos, blog posts, or any kind of social media you can imagine, and that content and those links should be distributed to dozens of different places and scheduled far into the future.

The best marketers will schedule and post their book links and content to the major social media sites that include Facebook, Twitter, LinkedIn, Google+, YouTube, Dailymotion, Vimeo, Tumblr, Pinterest, Instagram and cross-post between services.

But who has time for all of that scheduling, posting and reposting? Frankly, it's a giant pain and most people never set it up or take full advantage of the free marketing the big social media sites give you because it's overwhelming. Read on to find out how to overcome that obstacle...

Tool #3 is the **Perpetual Marketing Machine** that solves all those problems for you. It automates the posting, reposting and scheduling of your content so you can "set it once" and forget it.

You can set up and send out your videos, podcasts, articles, pictures, links of anything and the machine will put them on any site multiple times per day so you don't have to.

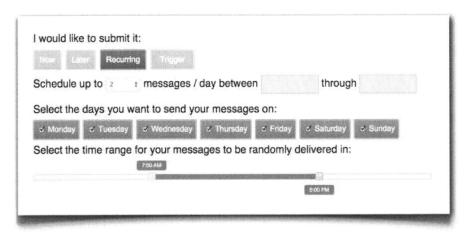

Another great way to promote your book is to put the content from your book into multiple formats, and redistribute or reuse it. The common term for this is "repurposing." You can actually publish various chapters of your book as blog postings or on Facebook. You can start a podcast on Apple iTunes and teach each of your chapters as podcast episodes.

You can also turn your book into a slideshow and distribute it on sites like SlideShare. And of course, each chapter can easily be a video that can be distributed on the major video networks like YouTube, Dailymotion, Vimeo, and on Facebook too.

Tool #3, the **Perpetual Marketing Machine** simplifies distribution for you.

Your goal is to get ATTENTION – everywhere, and capture leads.

If your reaction to hearing this is, "Why would anyone buy my book if they can get it for free in so many places and formats?" Good question.

Your goal is to capture eyeballs and imaginations, and get as much attention as you possibly can for as long as possible. These days, there's so much noise and overwhelm in the world that even if someone sees your book, another shiny object will appear seconds later and distract that person.

Your goal is to ENGAGE someone as quickly as possible - and if you can get them to take some kind of action to follow you on social media, buy your book on an impulse, subscribe to your podcast, register for a newsletter, watch of video of you on YouTube, then you've reached the first step in a new relationship...

Don't be afraid to give away your book in any format. Different types of people consume content in different formats or on different channels. Someone who finds out about you on iTunes might not be the same person who buys an e-book in Kindle format. That same person who reads about you on Facebook will not necessarily be the same person who reads a 140-character post on Twitter, or an article on LinkedIn. Different types of readers and consumers visit or prefer different social sites. The bottom line is your book becomes a marketing road map that allows you to repurpose and schedule your content, and create a conversation and an attention-getter for you.

It is also extremely effective for getting traditional media attention. Think of your book as a "media playbook" or "marketing roadmap" that a podcast, radio, or a television host or a producer can quickly look through for show ideas and things they can interview you about.

Imagine if a producer spots your book cover when they're browsing on Amazon or walking through a bookstore and examines your book. He or she glances at the title and subtitle and immediately understands the book's promise, who it is for, the problem it solves, and the big promise. They may decide to book you for an interview or a show, and want you to talk about something that is in chapter two or chapter seven.

Your book is a conversation starter that someone can have with you and think about you without you having to be there. Your goal is to get it in front of as many people as possible.

Ultimately, instead of being concerned about how many people are buying your book, focus on getting leads. You really don't need to care if it's read or consumed. It's more important that it generates an interactive, engaged conversation, or meeting with you that results in someone buying your product and services without caring whether or not there's a competitor or not. It is the most powerful way to build a high quality, high value relationship that can become extremely profitable.

Don't get me wrong, you and I both PREFER that they read our book because an indoctrinated reader will be a better-informed and educated prospect and customer. And the more they read, the more likely they are to buy and consume your more expensive products and services. Your banker isn't going to care if your $10,000 or $100,000 deposit came from someone who read your whole book. Neither will the charity of your choice when you write out a check for $25,000 because your book multiplied your income. You shouldn't either.

When you're easy to find, easy to reach, easy to engage on any device, anywhere, anytime, more people are going to find you, buy your products, services, media and speaking engagements and more profitable opportunities are going to appear for you.

Make sure you try out each of the marketing machines to see how they work!

CHAPTER FOURTEEN

Step #5—Profit

"Profit is the payoff of successful action."

Ludwig von Mises

In a survey and poll we recently did with 916 respondents, over 70% wanted to know how to promote, market and sell their books, and over 60% wanted to know how to build a list with a book. In a recent Forbes Magazine article, between 600,000 to 1,000,000 books are published every year in the United States alone, but most sell fewer than 250 copies over their lifetime depending on the distribution method. That means and translates into about $750 to $2,000 in royalty payments to the author.

What the heck!?!?

Given the time that it takes for most people to write, publish, promote, get deals and all the expenses involved preparing and writing a book, the lost income and opportunities, those people would be better off getting a part-time job at McDonalds and probably make substantially more money. But in a recent test that we did teaching the Publish and Profit System, out of 39 people who went through the course, 26 published, promoted, and became bestselling authors in fewer than three weeks. Many of them wound up getting substantial business deals and attention in the media because of it including Winnie Anderson who closed a $2,043 and $5,000 deal in less than a week because of her book.

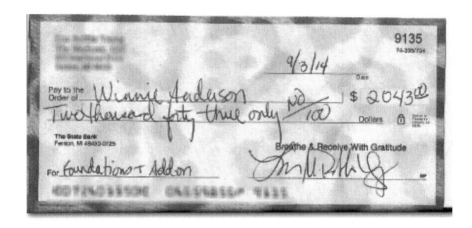

If it hasn't become obvious by now, the money you make in publishing isn't from *royalty checks*. This model isn't about selling books. It's about the "back end" and what your book will give you. It's the access it provides, it's the doors it opens, it's the business opportunities, the interviews in the media and the social value and gravitas a book provides.

Yes, you can make money with royalties - and some people do. According to a press release Amazon made recently they said 150 Kindle Direct Publishing (KDP) authors each sold more than 100,000 copies of their books in 2013. There are nearly five million Kindle titles listed for sale, and of course there are millions of other books too.

Now, chances are you and I probably won't be in that list of 150 who sell 100,000 copies. But when we include a call to action (CTA) and include a "Crowd Grabber" or a reason for people to respond inside our book, the model gets very interesting. In my personal experience, I've found that for every 10 books I sell on Amazon, I get about four leads.

That not might sound like much, but anytime you get a lead that is a book buyer, even if it's for $0.99-$2.99, it's still a motivated and qualified prospect. And if you have a business offering or a product or service you can sell, and send that lead into a marketing funnel where you educate or speak with that prospect and convince them to buy a product or service, you can make a lot of money.

In my experience, the value of a lead is anywhere between $27 all the way up to $100 or more. I would much rather make a $100 each time I sold a $0.99 Kindle book, wouldn't you? That sure beats the heck out of $0.30 or $2 royalty per book! Why not earn money multiple ways?

In the next chapter, we're going to review 11 different ways to profit from your book. This is just a small number of different strategies and techniques we and our customers and clients are using to earn more, live more and give more!

11 Ways to Profit From Your Book

---

*"Don't let the fear of losing be greater than
the excitement of winning."*
Robert Kiyosaki

*"The only point in making money is so you can tell
some big shot where to go."*
Humphrey Bogart

"Carpe per diem – seize the check."
Robin Williams

A book is all about bridging the credibility gap between marketing and authenticity. It's a very powerful way to create that conversation; whether you're on stage and people get to see you, through your book or through automated conversations in your marketing.

I've never publicly mentioned this before, but I met my wife years ago on a trip to Greece. The trip lasted three weeks. On that trip we got to know each other very well. I was completely impressed and blown away with her. I not only admired her, but I also envied her *because she was a published author*. Professionally she worked for one of my great mentors, Deepak Chopra, M.D., and a dozen bestselling authors doing marketing for them.

When she told the story about how she watched Deepak (and Deepak is one of the most prolific writers ever - he's written close to 100 books), she said, "I watched all these people and I finally had that moment where I said 'I can do this, too. I'm going to write and publish a book'." This was 20 years ago when writing and publishing books meant getting an agent, doing a book tour and getting media trained.

Her first book is called *Twelve Lessons on Life I Learned from my Garden: Spiritual Guidance from the Vegetable Patch.*

I fell in love with her **because of her book**. I found and heard a side of her soul that I could not find any other way. I already knew she was smart, I knew she was deep, and I knew she was complex. There's never a dull moment with Vivian. She's always *interesting and interested.*

But the book changed everything for me…and I saw her from a completely different perspective. When I found out she was a published author, I saw her as if she was a celebrity. After reading the book, something else changed. I got to know her from her own narrative – and after a few hours of reading, it seemed as though we had spent years getting to know each other.

That's the opportunity when you write a book. You have a way to express yourself, share ideas and feelings that can only be expressed through writing. You have more time to think about what you're going to share. Best of all, you can control the narrative and communicate years or decades worth of ideas and experiences in a few short hours.

I can't promise you'll find or marry a spouse because of your book. But what I can promise is there are lots of ways to profit from your book. It's certainly possible that you prospects will fall in *like* (maybe even love) with you because of your book!

Here are 11 ways to profit from your book:

Book Profit Opportunity #1: Royalties

I recently received a $1,600 royalty check from one of my books. That's great. But there's a lot more money in the leads you get from your books.

As soon as you upload your book to Amazon, you'll start getting paid every 30 days after your book starts selling. When you publish to the other platforms like Bookbaby, Nook, Cobo, Copia, Garner's Books, Baker & Taylor, Centra, Scribd, Flipkart, Oyster, Ossiano, and Barnes and Noble, you'll make more. Amazon puts the money right into your bank account. Yummy.

We show you all the different ways and places to get published in the Publish and Profit course and how to do it too.

Contrary to what most authors do, I usually set my book prices to the lowest possible rate - even if I'm earning almost no royalties. To me, the value of the lead is considerably higher than the royalty. I'd rather have the LEADS than the few bucks I can make on the book sale. That's because a lead can be worth $25-$100 to me once they go through our marketing funnel as opposed to $0.35-$7.00 royalty.

That lead is worth five to ten times more over the long term when they invest in our products, services and memberships.

Once you've built a list from your books and the exposure your book gives you and have a history of selling lots of copies (if that's your goal), you can always get signed up with a literary agent who can sell a book idea to a major publishing house and possibly get an advance.

My friend JJ Virgin received a multimillion-dollar advance for her new book, "The Sugar Impact Diet" and the "Sugar Impact Diet Cookbook." Those kinds of deals happen after you've written and self-published a couple books and are a proven winner.

In the Publish and Profit course, we include presentations with two well known NY Literary Agents, Celeste Fine and Scott Hoffman. Celeste is JJ's book agent. Both are known for getting large six and seven-figure advances for the authors they work with.

By self-publishing a couple books, you prepare yourself for that kind of payday in the future. It's extremely rare nowadays for a previously unpublished author who doesn't have a large database and social following to receive an advance unless they're a celebrity.

Book Profit Opportunity #2: Licensing

One of our clients, Karol Clark, has a business with her husband. They're in the surgical weight loss business.

After Karol wrote three books that are used to generate leads for their business, she also created marketing materials that help them grow their business too.

It turns out many doctors in their business aren't good marketers (actually, most doctors are terrible marketers). Karol had a great idea - she started licensing her marketing materials and content to other doctors! By doing so, she was able to earn a substantial amount of money selling to her competitors!

Another strategy you could use is to write a book about a product or service you really like. For example, if you are a big fan of Evernote, you could write the equivalent of "Evernote for Dummies" and fill it with lots of great tips and strategies.

If Evernote or another company you write a book for has an affiliate program, you can include links to their service, other products and services that support that product and make money as an affiliate with links in your "Call to Action" bonuses at the end of each book chapter.

You can also license or sell your book to the company for an annual fee.

You can sell your own products or consulting services by leveraging a major name brand in the title or subtitle of your book! Once you start thinking about the possibilities, there are lots of ways to earn money with a "hybrid" licensing model.

Book Profit Opportunity #3: Audiobooks

Have you ever imagined your book being sold on Apple's iTunes store, on the Audible.com site, on Amazon's audio store? How awesome would it be for people to be able to listen to you on their phones, in cars, tablets or computers? Maybe you haven't thought of it before - but it's easier that you might imagine.

Amazon has a program called Audio Creation Exchange (ACX) that helps you sell an audio version of your book. They'll pay you 40% to 50% commissions or even higher if someone downloads your audiobook. If they become an audible subscriber, they give you an extra $50 bonus for that.

You get free Audible Amazon and iTunes distribution immediately with ACX. Did I mention it's free? You continue to own and control everything; and, you can take it down whenever you want. And the visibility that an audiobook gives you can be very considerable in search engines.

What's really important is audio books are another DISTRIBUTION CHANNEL. More channels equals more customers and more exposure. Book listeners are often very different than book buyers. It's a way to reach even more people in a very, very intimate fashion.

Two of my good friends are dyslexic and not big readers because they can't read quickly. However, they are voracious audiobook consumers – and big buyers. If you don't have an audio book, there's a strong chance you'll never reach a certain audience!

The great thing is you don't have to come up with new content. All you do is read or record the content of your book and you have a new product to sell online and get paid immediately with no overhead.

And just like your Kindle and paperback, your audio book becomes a lead generator for you too.

If you don't know how to record the audio yourself or don't know anything about audio production or distribution, Amazon can handle getting your book recorded. They'll help you find the talent.

Inside Amazon's ACX program, there are lists of producers and audio voiceover talent that will narrate your book for you.

Here's a bonus idea for you: inside your book, offer to give away an audio version of your book for free when they text their email address to you using the "Crowd Capture" Marketing Machine. It's a great bonus and perfect incentive for someone to take action and invite you into their ears, pockets, cars or home!

Book Profit Opportunity #4: Sales and Opt-ins

I'm probably going to sound like a broken record (and make a reference to an obsolete technology at the same time), but here goes.

- You can package YOU, your ideas, expertise, know-how, wisdom, and diagnostic tools into a book.
- Several of the biggest brands in the world including Amazon, Apple and Google will sell your book FOR FREE and pay you 70% commissions
- The biggest social media networks will promote and market your book and whatever content you make FOR FREE and make you accessible to 73% of the human race
- Your book content can be repurposed into podcasts, videos, articles, slides, pictures, articles
- Your book can give you access to big media, interviews and celebrity status
- You can passionately brag and talk about your products and services
- And anyone who buys that book has proven to you that they are a BUYER and interested in exactly what you're talking about and the results you promise them
- And you can incentivize those readers to give you their name, email address, phone number and physical address so you can…
- Sell them you your products and services!

Hello! Is this really happening? REALLY?

Seriously, this is the best thing that's happened to civilized man since Eve. Or maybe the wheel. Or the toilet. Dang, I don't know, but it's really good.

Product sales are the single most lucrative way to make money from your book. I've consistently produced over $1,000,000 in sales of my products from the last six books I've written within 100 days and I'm not special – just committed and motivated.

I think of a book as a fun, informative, storytelling sales letter (when it's done right). You can give great value while building your credibility and building a relationship with the reader. Hopefully you feel that way about me and the information I'm sharing with you right now.

Every single chapter should drive the reader to an opt-in for a different reason. Every chapter is a different conversation; it's a different story with a reason and a purpose. Your job is to show your reader opportunities, possibilities and potential.

For example, when you respond to one of the links in this book, text your email address or fill out your information, you'll get free video training that teaches and demonstrates these powerful concepts. In one of the videos, we share success stories from all walks of life.

We show you real people and evidence - that's physical, irrefutable proof we know what we're talking about, this is real and it works.

I challenge you to name anything that a book can't sell; I certainly can't think of one thing. It is an unbelievable platform for promotion, branding and sales.

Again, I'll shamelessly be a self-promoter and tell you to visit www.PublishAndProfit.com to watch our videos, try out some of the exercises, participate in the community, fill out a survey and try out the program.

Everything I've been sharing with you in this book is real and it works!

Book Profit Opportunity #5: Consulting

We've trained hundreds of consultants over the last 24 months how to write, publish and promote books for business owners. And we've found, the ultimate positioning and authority tool for them to close deals is with a book of their own.

Instead of repeating what's already been said, go back and re-read chapter 4 for the "Top 10 Reasons to Write a Book" because now that you've been through the process, you'll see how all of these things come together:

- Reason #1: It's an instant credibility booster
- Reason #2: A perfect "foot in the door strategy"
- Reason #5: A perfect way to position yourself as a consultant or authority
- Reason #6: Writing books is a great way to get speaking opportunities
- Reason #8: A book can build your local business
- Reason #10: Published authors make more money and help more people

Ed Rush is a prime example of this. One of his books, *How to Turn Clicks into Clients* created a 6-figure business working with attorneys. Every time he presented, he gave his book away and then people in the audience would approach him and ask if he recommended that they work with his company.

THAT'S positioning!

In our bonus interviews in an upcoming chapter, you'll meet several of our customers who are all using books as ways to grow their consulting businesses and earn substantially more income because of a book.

By the way, if you're a consultant (or want to make money with what you know), we have a super 4-part video course on how to get up, running, and profitable. It's at

www.TopGunToolkit.com.

Book Profit Opportunity #6: Interviews

If you want to get to know celebrities and influential people, the fastest way to do that is with a book. All you do is email or call them and ask if you can interview them for your book on (Insert topic). In our experience, they say yes - almost every time.

Why? Well, first, everyone has an ego. And the idea of being interviewed is appealing. Second, just like you, they're probably looking for more exposure too. So you're actually doing them a favor.

The interview starts a relationship that can lead to consulting, more deals, long term relationships, open doors and more.

For people who have followings and a list, help them sell their products. You'll be surprised at what happens when you help them make money. They'll return the favor!

Now, you have to "walk up the ladder" - in other words, you aren't going to get to Brad Pitt, Tom Cruise or Arianna Huffington when you're just starting out. You'll start with other authors, business people you respect and eventually work your way "up the food chain" once you've proven yourself as a good interviewer and won't damage their reputation.

It does take practice and perseverance, but every celebrity started out as a nobody and just kept asking until they reached the finish line!

There are two magic sentences that help you get your foot in the door and get access to the people you want to reach:

Magic sentence #1 - find someone you want to interview, even a famous person and reach out to him or her or their assistant. The magic sentence is "can I interview you on my show?"

If your goal is to pick up a consulting client or deal, you can use…

Magic sentence #2 - "I have an idea about how you can grow your business." After your interview ends, you have rapport and trust built up with the interviewee. Now is the time to share some ideas with them - which can include your consulting services, coaching or products.

Magic sentence #3 - "Will you introduce me to three other people I should interview that you respect and are a good fit for this format?" This is a very powerful question and a great way to move up that proverbial food chain!

Book Profit Opportunity #7: Speaking Gigs

Your book can be invaluable in helping you book paid speaking gigs. Think about it - if you're planning a meeting and you have a $5,000 budget, who would you prefer to hire as a speaker - an unknown or an expert and authority who is also a #1 bestselling author?

When you speak, you're most likely going to be speaking to high value audiences. These are people who are paying thousands of dollars, potentially tens of thousands of dollars, just to be there. They're away from their business, their families, they're paying for the event, travel, hotel, food and most likely, not making money while they are away.

Most likely, they're looking for a business opportunity, personal breakthrough, new tools, strategies, networking with new people or resources to make more and add more value to their business or life.

Speaking also gives you the opportunity to sell your books and products from the stage.

I regularly "convert" 10%-50% of an audience of 150-600 people into buyers of my $2,000 products with a 75 minute speech. That's $50,000-$100,000 per HOUR or more in income!

Here's another example:

My former business partner, Dean Hyers teaches corporate audiences how to speak and present authentically. His corporate customers pay him anywhere from $10,000 to $35,000 to be trained by his company, SagePresence.

The way he used to get clients and deals was to speak to corporate audiences. The problem was, event producers were resistant when he told them he charged $5,000-$7,000 to speak. Most had the same response "we don't have a speaking budget."

I've been telling him for years, "Dean, write a book – it'll sell for you." For years, he pushed back because the timing didn't "feel right" to him, that it would take too much time, that he didn't have months to block out and quick working, etc. I told him about our process and system. I shared with him some ideas that I was certain would help him get more clients and make more money.

That pushed him over the top – he was committed, had a clear plan and an incentive to move forward.

He finally wrote his book over a period of a few months. Next, he wanted to become a #1 Bestselling Author - he knew that would help him get more speaking opportunities so he asked for my advice.

The way he reached #1 bestseller was really simple. Dean hosted a book launch party, invited friends, customers, clients to that room and he asked them all to buy the book on Amazon right there in the room from their phones. It only took about 100 sales to send him up to #1. My community of customers also got behind him and bought his book too, which kept him on #1 for almost two weeks.

That gave Dean celebrity status - "#1 Bestselling Author" which is a title he has for the rest of his life.

Here's how he started making money with his book.

Based on my advice, he turned his book into a $300 how-to product. (Remember - the book is the WHAT, the product is the HOW).

Now, every time he went to the organizer of a speaking event, they'd always say, "Well, we don't have a budget for speaking."

He would say, "Do you have a training budget?"

They'd say, "Yes, of course we have a training budget."

He'd say, "Great. How many people are going to be in the room at the event?"

"100 People."

Dean will say, "Here's what I'll do. My product is $300, buy the program for all 100 people who will be in the audience, I'll throw in 100 books and speak for free."

One simple shift in strategy quadrupled his speaking fee to $30,000!

He not only gets paid more, every single person in the room receives his book and product. The book indoctrinates them; the product indoctrinates them; and a lot of attendees walk up to him after his presentation and say, "I don't have time to go through the product, will you just come to our offices and train us in person?"

As a result of this strategy, Dean is making more money, booking more speaking gigs at $15,000 to $35,000 and he's closing more deals too!

How's that for a million dollar idea?

Book Profit Opportunity #8: Community and Events

One of our customers, John C. sells products and services that teach real estate investors how to get investment money without credit.

He wrote a book about the process he uses and then turned the book into a $3,500 course.

Every two weeks, he schedules an event on www.MeetUp.com and offers to give away a copy of his book for anyone who signs up.

Then at the meetup, he talks to people, brainstorms with them and ultimately, sells them his course.

He also has produced a webinar so anyone who buys his book can register for the free training webinar. It's the same presentation he makes at the meetup groups, but online.

Producing your own event is very powerful way to generate a lot of income especially when you have a highly qualified audience. If you're in front of an audience that has spent time and money to be there, you can collect leads or even sell products.

You can use your book to drive attendees to online or offline events.

In our programs, we host live events several times per year. We teach, train, bring in successful customers who share their tips and strategies on panels and do "hot seats" where we consult with people in front of the live audience about how to use and implement our products to improve their businesses.

Events represent the ultimate means of fulfillment. This is where you actually get to connect and touch your tribe and your following. It's also a perfect place to launch a new product or book.

Book Profit Opportunity #9: Product Launches

A book is a perfect way to educate and touch a prospect and indoctrinate them into a "product launch". It is also an extremely effective way to release a new product and generate lots of sales in a short period of time and it can work for any business type - not just online.

Over the past 6 years, we've produced 12 consecutive multi-million dollar product launches. 6 out of 12 began by giving away a book.

Giving away a book as a lead generator is a perfect way to provide a high-quality reason for someone to give you their email address and name.

It's also a great way to get JV partners and affiliates to get involved because they're giving away your book as a bonus to their list. Books are perceived as high-quality giveaways.

This is an example of an email I send to get people to optin for a product launch sequence:

```
Subject: Get my new book free!

I just released my new book, "Publish and Profit: A 5
Step System For Attracting Paying Coaching & Consulting
```

Clients, Traffic & Leads, Product Sales and Speaking Engagements" and you can get it for free for the next couple of days.

It's right here at **www.PublishAndProfit.com**

In the book, I share:

- What I've found to be single most powerful marketing tool in the world
- What I would do right now if I were starting a new business from scratch
- The 10 reasons why this is the best way to market any business (or your brand)
- The ONE THING I'd do differently if I were starting a new business from scratch. It's also my biggest professional regret.

You don't want to miss out on getting this - I'll be taking it down after this weekend.

Mike

PS - In addition to the book, I'm also including video versions of the book too. It's packed with useful content and ideas you can use right now in your business.

=======

This works so well because you're giving REAL value...and not just fluff.

We also found that books are a great giveaway when you advertise on Facebook. A real book means your opt-in ratio is going to be very high so you pay less for your leads.

Books not only help your positioning and the bragging rights, but Amazon is promoting you; elevating your visibility; showing your book is on the bestseller fast track. All it's going to do is bring more people who are highly motivated and highly qualified into your product launch.

If you're not already going through our "Launch Sequence", make sure you register at www.PublishAndProfit.com and you can watch our videos and participate in the community.

There's also an opportunity to brainstorm a book title and subtitle and get a book cover made for your book idea!

Book Profit Opportunity #10: Webcasts

Live interactive video is the most effective way to sell products and services online. Period.

If you learn how to do it, you can make hundreds of thousands or millions of dollars and it costs nothing except for basic computer equipment.

I'm biased - and I'll be the first to admit that selling with live interactive video is one of my "superpowers" - I've been doing it now since 2007 when it was extremely complicated and expensive. I've spent years studying and crafting my skills to sell with online video.

We regularly sell upwards of $50,000-$250,000 or even more worth of products during a single live interactive show in front of hundreds or thousands of viewers.

There are many affordable ways to do webcasts - the easiest and cheapest is with Google Hangouts. You can just open up your laptop, turn on your webcam and start broadcasting to one or hundreds of thousands of people at a time for FREE.

Ten years ago, this was practically impossible to do and would cost millions of dollars. This technology is rapidly making satellite and broadcast television systems obsolete. I believe in this platform so much that I've bet my future on it.

We use a higher-end, but still free "big brother" to Google Hangouts, YouTube Live.

It requires more hardware and training to make it work - we have a $750,000 studio with eight sets, eight cameras and it's computer controlled, but the fact is, you don't need fancy equipment or a lot of training to make money with a webcast.

With webcasts, you can do "live video book tours", training events or sales events.

Webcasts can be adapted to virtually any business type. The key to making them work is to be interesting, entertaining, mix the right amount of education and super interactive.

If you haven't attended one of our webcasts, make sure you register below and you'll be sent a notification for our next one. They're lots of fun and it's a great chance for you and I get to get to know each other virtually!

WATCH AND LEARN MORE ABOUT WEBCASTS

To get a copy of my ninth #1 bestselling book, "The Webcast Profit Toolkit" and an interactive training video about webcasting and how you can use it to start or grow a business, build an engaged audience and list, create products, share your message with the world and meet other abundance-minded entrepreneurs, small business owners, authors, experts, speakers, consultants and coaches

Visit www.WebcastProfitToolkit.com

Book Profit Opportunity #11: Affiliate and JV Promotions

If you're not familiar with affiliate promotions, they're pretty simple. A company or individual will pay you a referral fee or commission when you sell their products. It's a "pay for performance" model. Amazon for example, pays commissions if you send someone to Amazon to buy a product you recommend with a link.

Fortunately, there are LOTS of great companies and products you can sell and earn great commissions or you can make arrangements with companies who will gladly pay you if you help them grow their businesses.

Think about it. A book is the ultimate credibility and authority-building tool and when someone is reading what you write, they'll believe your recommendations too. So, find some products that you really believe in and link to them in your book.

You can also use webcasts to feature affiliate, JV or client products and services and sell them from the comfort of your home or office.

Here's a big POWER TIP for you and a way to supercharge your book-based affiliate promotions, build a list and make a name for yourself at the same time.

The BEST way to generate traffic, leads and affiliate sales is to create chapters in your book about a specific strategy, tactic, outcome or result that the reader is interested in. Describe in detail how to accomplish that and make a step-by-step video that demonstrates how to do that action.

At the end of every chapter, tell the reader that they can get that demonstration video and all the other ones in the book for free when they visit your web site or Crowd Grabber campaign.

This can work for healthcare, nutrition, weight loss, financial products, coaching, consulting, tools and training - literally anything.

This way, you build massive value in your book, there's a logical reason for your reader to give you their contact information in exchange for some valuable ongoing training.

Better yet - because YOU are capturing that lead directly instead of passing it to someone else, if you decide you want to recommend a different product or make your own at some point, you'll have your own list to market and promote to!

I earn enough money every month from affiliate and JV promotions to pay my house mortgage and car payment from promotions I ran over a year ago.

CHAPTER SIXTEEN

Summary

That wraps up the different ways to make money with your book. With a little more time, I could probably come up with 20-30 more but this should get your "gears spinning" inside your head and you'll likely think of several ways you can adapt these strategies for your business.

You can certainly join us during one of our interactive webcasts and ask us questions too. Just make sure you register to get more information and videos.

As a parting shot, I'll tell you this - you only need to implement 1 or 2 of these ideas to create a really nice income stream for yourself. Trying to do all of them is a recipe for doing nothing! So pick one and get started. One of the fastest ways to the cash is to simply use a book to position you as a consultant...and then close deals.

Also, as you create and publish books, you'll come up with some moneymaking ideas yourself. So keep the list going! This isn't exclusive. There are probably thousands of ways to monetize your book, but none of them work if you're sitting on your butt. Get going and get into action...then send us your results so we can make you famous!

Speaking of implementing, read on. You're about to find out how to get this done QUICKLY.

CHAPTER SEVENTEEN

Are You Interested or Committed?

"The only limit to your impact is your imagination and commitment."

Anthony Robbins

Now that you've been exposed to a variety of different ways to make money when you write your book, I would like to invite you to watch several videos that will introduce you to the opportunity of writing a book - and benefitting from the things that we've discussed.

These videos will reveal a step-by-step process for how to get your book published, inspiring case studies of other people and our clients and customers who have written, published, promoted, and became #1 bestselling authors, and an opportunity to see a step-by-step system that will show you how to do it and include one-on-one coaching and support to creating a beautiful and attractive book cover, software tools to help you write and create a winning book title, a done-for-you book selling website and a website that captures leads and automates your marketing for you too.

There's also a fantastic Facebook group filled with like-minded and abundance-minded entrepreneurs and experts who all support each other by buying each other's books, providing book title and book cover feedback, and are constantly testing and trying out new strategies for building a list, growing their business, and making money with books.

YOU'RE ALMOST THERE!

Chuck Yeager was the first person to break the sound barrier.
Here's what he said:

"At the moment of truth, there are either reasons or results."

Are you ready for your breakthrough?

YOU can be a published author in just a few weeks.

Visit **www.PublishAndProfit.com/BookBonus**
or text your email address to (858) 707-7417

CHAPTER EIGHTEEN

Meet Five Successful Publish & Profit Authors

"The successful warrior is the average man, with laser-like focus."

Bruce Lee

Two of my favorite things I really enjoy doing are:

1. Interviewing smart, successful people
2. Celebrating my customer's successes

When I get to do both at the same time, it's a dream-come-true. That's what you'll experience in these final chapters.

Each of these five people have real businesses and they're using the power of our Publish and Profit system to have real impact and change lives.

What I hope you take away from these interviews is a combination of possibility, hope, inspiration, motivation and mindset and experience what they've accomplished and can enjoy the same rewards they are!

One important note: these are transcripts from video interviews I did during a live event. Aside from some grammatical tweaks, they're untouched. There are colloquial phrases and references made to some pictures we were showing on a screen. The point of including these interviews is to illustrate some of the remarkable things that can happen to you when you write a book or become a published author just like them.

I chose this small group of people because they're all abundance-minded members of our community who give first and ask second. They serve a higher purpose and have the mindset and psychology of winners and leaders.

Enjoy them - and when you've finished reading, make sure you sign up for the free video series. The third video includes more interviews with other successful members of our community. Real people doing really cool things and getting paid too!

Interview #1: Everett O'Keefe - How a Bestselling Book Launched Real Consulting Business

Mike Koenigs: Meet Everett O'Keefe. He is a remarkable human being and he's got a great story to share with you about just what has been going on in his life, his business, his career and his family. Everett, why don't you just start and share?

Everett O'Keefe: I got involved in this community about 18 months ago at a live event and started your training with some really incredible people, with big hearts and genius ideas; it helps to have both. It has really been outstanding.

But I didn't come here from an easy place. My business partner, John Riding, and me were scraping by; really scraping by. We were selling text message marketing to retail businesses and we thought it was a big deal if we found a client that would pay us $80 a month. We thought that was great. That came off the back of doing a bunch of network marketing together, of which we found we had no gift for whatsoever. We love working with businesses and we had some really great clients.

But I found myself waking up at about three in the morning - and I am not an early riser. I woke up thinking, "Okay, how am I going to pay that bill? How am I going to handle this? What am I going to do next?" It seemed like a couple of months of waking up on that schedule saying, "Oh, this is just killing me!"

We had a great client, a guy named Frank Leyes, who is a certified financial planner, speaker and now an author. He had invited me to one of your events. He said, "Hey, what do you think about this Koenigs guy?" I had been following you for a while and I said, "You know what? Let's go to your event; because Mike combines strategies with tools and with sincerity." And that's something that isn't common. So we came… and I'm so glad we did. It was fantastic; I learned a lot. I went back to the office right after one of the events and I told my business partner, John, "John: two things. We're writing a book. You didn't know this, but we're going to write a book today. And John, by the way, I signed us up for a certification program that cost more than we have made last year." We hadn't made much. And John said, "Oh, really? Okay."

So we wrote our first book, *The Video Tractor Beam*. It was about video marketing, something that we knew more about than most of the people we talked to. We sat down, used your system, dictated it and had it transcribed… and 30 days later, we did an Amazon launch and took it to #1. It was one of those things where I saw people on your stage and I said to myself, "Okay, I want to do that. That's cool!" And I knew I wanted to help my clients write books too. But if we were going to do it for clients, I wanted to test it. I wanted to make sure it worked. And when I first saw our ranking actually come up on the board on Amazon with more than 100, I was like, "John, it's in the top 100!" and then pretty soon, I was saying, "It's in the top 20!" and then, "John, it's #1! How cool is that?"

Mike Koenigs: "Quick! Take a screen snapshot of that #1 position and save it now!" [This is important – we always want to capture the book when it reaches a #1 bestseller so we have proof for marketing and positioning purposes]

Publish And Profit: A 5-Step System For Attracting Paying Coaching And Consulting Clients, Traffic And Leads,... by Mike Koenigs and Ed Rush (Oct 2, 2014)

$0.99 Kindle Edition
Auto-delivered wirelessly

 In Business Leadership Training

Books: See all he...

11 Days from an Idea to Published, Profitable and Reaching #1 Bestseller! :) Thank You!

Everett O'Keefe: Yes. Oh yeah. Trust me, we were doing screenshots all the way.

We didn't realize how transformative it would be professionally and personally. It was really incredible because as a result of writing the book, we started having people come up to us, "Hey, I saw your post on Facebook!" or "I bought a copy of your book!" A guy walked up up to my business partner John at a restaurant and said, "Hey, aren't you a bestselling author or something like that?" Another guy came up to him one time and said, "Aren't you kind of a big deal?" It was just that kind of stuff... and it was really weird because I think what gets lost in the shuffle is that when we launch books, you're suddenly treated very differently.

After a while, people start telling you, "Wow, you're a big deal!" And yes, you start to understand that people see authors in a really special way. There is really nothing like it. As a result, you start to posture differently; stand a little taller when you're talking to a business owner. You're not just schlepping text messaging for $80 a month. Now you're providing them with a way that they can market themselves better. You're turning people into stars. It really was transformative for us.

Mike Koenigs: So what happened next?

Everett O'Keefe: We decided if we could become a #1 bestselling author, we could write, publish and promote books for others. And people started coming out of the woodwork that needed books, some of them are here in this room. And it kind of goes like this: because we wrote a book, we could help others get their message out. For instance, I could help a guy who is already an expert at Amazon marketing really leverage that and help explode his business. Because we wrote a book, I could help a friend who had his lifelong desire to write a business book and get an Amazon #1 in business networking. Because we wrote a book, I could help a speaker become an author and help transform the way America spends and saves.

Mike Koenigs: And that is Frank Leyes, the guy who introduced us.

Everett O'Keefe: Yes, absolutely. And because we wrote a book, we could help save America's crumbling roadways and the different ways that America's infrastructure is built, by helping Blair Bernhardt.

Mike Koenigs: Who you met in our community?

Everett O'Keefe: Who we met here, that's exactly right. In fact, he did a hot seat at one of your events with you guys. Because we wrote a book, we could help a very successful businessman inspire people to elevate and to really find their greatness. Because of a book, we could help people create Christ-centered marriages. Because of a book, we could help a worship team at a church launch an album that made it onto the billboard top 50 and was in the top 60 on iTunes in all albums and the top 50 in Amazon in all albums. Because of a book, we could help a pastor of a church get out his message about living a God-centered life.

Mike Koenigs: Here they are (shows pictures of all the books they've written).

Everett O'Keefe: And it's all because he started with a book for us, a little book. It's not just that; we could have done all of those things - but it just would never have happened if I hadn't come to an event and watched people with their books and said, "Man, I think I'd like to try that." It all started there. As a result, we've been able to help carry other people's messages to the world. That's all because of a book.

Mike Koenigs: Wow! Let's talk about the people.

Everett O'Keefe: There is a special guy on the screen right now. Well, I'm not even going to call him my former business partner; he is still my business partner. But my best friend, John Riding, who I started this business with, he has been absolutely amazing. Many of you know that John passed away literally during our last event playing volleyball; he had a massive heart attack.

Amazing things have come as a result, amazing things. One of them was at your last event where I was surrounded by a circle of people praying for John and his family. And we've received incredible support from this community. It's really been inspiring. And because of some, quite honestly, God-orchestrated events before and after his death, that was the worst and best time of my life. I couldn't have gotten through it in any way like I had without the community that has been built right here with really, really incredible people.

So, John is still my business partner. And his family and I are in close touch and awesome. And I think just an example of what happened there are the type of people, Mike, that you've brought together into this community. I'm so glad they dragged him into a book and a certification.

It's really been great. But because of a book, I could do some really awesome things with my best friend in business and have an amazing time with it; but also develop an amazing community. This is a picture from our Mastermind retreat we did in Yosemite, and how we work together as a community to support each other. Actually, a bunch of you were there, which was really, really great; and it's just where we all came together to build each other's businesses; to strengthen each other and to develop community and family. Because of a book, this could happen for anyone.

But for me, I have to tell you, it comes down to my family. Because of a book, I can support my family. I didn't have to wake up at three in the morning wondering how I was going to pay the bills. I sometimes wake up at three in the morning wondering how I'm going to do everything I'm going to do for my clients, I do. But I absolutely love my work; I absolutely love it. In fact, I never come home burned out or tired because I'm always working to help really incredible people and it's a blast.

And really, you and your team have helped give me a model for a business, a tool for it, a community to support it, strategies to execute it and just guidance all along the way, through a combination of live events and certifications and an online community, as well as an in-touch community.

As a result, here's the deal. I can go to my son Connor's water polo games whenever I want. I can go to my daughter's swimming. I can go to Kyle's (my youngest son's) band performances. I can support my wife, I can support my kids, I can be there in their lives. And I'm not worried about a clock; I'm not worried about somebody's schedule; I don't have to ask anybody for any time off to make that happen. I can just go do it. I can be the dad that I really want to be. And it all started with a book.

Mike Koenigs: Beautiful! What a great life you have!

All right, we've got a few minutes left and we can kind of talk about the "doing" part - because that's what I know a lot of people want to know what else you've done and how you've done it.

I remember one of my favorite things about what you've done is not only did you come back from an event and you wrote the first book... I can remember one time when you left your second event, you guys learned about podcasting and you were very inspired. Do you want to tell that brief story?

Everett O'Keefe: Okay. Our model with everything is "What's the point of learning it if we can't execute it?" ...and that's the challenge to anybody who buys a product or attends an event; they spend a lot of money learning stuff and unfortunately fail to execute. So on the way back from one of your events in San Diego, we had a GoPro camera that we stuck it on the dash of the car. We're driving home in the dark on the I5 over the Grapevine. I don't recommend this, by the way. But we put on every dome light in the car and we recorded our first video podcast.

And we created the artwork; we did a voiceover; we posted it to iTunes; we did *everything* from the car. By the time we got home to Fresno (it's about a five and a half-hour drive), our podcast was live. Yeah, it's still there. It's not perfect. But if you want to see a couple of goofy guys try not to get pulled over by the highway patrol in the middle of the night driving home, you can go find it there.

Mike Koenigs: What did you call your podcast?

Everett O'Keefe: It was Road-casting.

Mike Koenigs: Road-casting.

Everett O'Keefe: Yes. We've patented that, as far as I know.

Mike Koenigs: That's fantastic. All right, but that really got things going. You got a book client.

Everett O'Keefe: Actually, you know what? This was a referral from your community. Todd Ramsey said, "Hey, I need to get a book out. I don't know how to do it; you just did one. Can you help me?" We said, "Well, I think we know how a little bit. So sure, absolutely, we can do it," and we did and got a #2 or #3 bestseller status. It helped revolutionized this guy's business, made Todd look really good too. And we were really happy to do that.

Everett O'Keefe: Then there's Beth. Beth is at a local networking Chamber of Commerce, she's awesome. She wanted to write this book and we said, "Yeah, we'll help you launch it." She had already written it. That's the other great thing; so many people will come to you with their books already written - they just need help launching. There's massive value in making that happen.

Mike Koenigs: And with Frank Leyes?

Everett O'Keefe: Frank had been writing a book for three years before we met. And about three years later, he actually finished it, with us driving him. Frank got ranked #1 in five categories on Amazon. You can only pick three: two with Kindle and one in Book; but he got five because he also dominated the parent categories of those subcategories. Frank's speaking revenue has gone up about 600% since that book was published a year ago.

Mike Koenigs: Right. Let's talk a little bit about certification; because you ended up going through our Publish and Profit certification course which shows you how to provide book writing and marketing services to clients as a business. Both of you did it or was it just you?

Everett O'Keefe: Yeah, actually, several now. I think we've gone through almost every certification that you've offered since we started; and those have been absolutely phenomenal. The strategies we learn at many of the live events; how to execute the strategies we learn in detail through certification. And that's been great, absolutely fantastic. And then, of course, I have met incredible people in the certified community. Gosh! I've got three different Masterminds - they all come from the certified community that we participate in and we all support each other through it. Certification has been the doorway. Quite frankly, that's what made it serious. That's what made it serious for us. It was, "Okay. We're going to invest the time and money. We're going to make it work. We're going to make it happen."

Mike Koenigs: Right. And I don't know this for sure, but did you finance your certification through a client project? How did that happen?

Everett O'Keefe: Yeah. So at the first event we went to, Ed Rush had spoken about certification and he challenged us. He said, "Hey, look, if you don't have the money, go find a client. Go get a client between now and the certification date. Tell him what you're going to do for them when certification is done, and go make it happen. Your client can pay for your certification and they'll be your first paying client at the same time." That's exactly what we did.

Mike Koenigs: Who was the client?

Everett O'Keefe: Actually, a realtor in our area. And it was a video marketing package, and that absolutely worked out.

Mike Koenigs: So you got the gig before you knew what you were going to do... and then you financed it... and then you came back and did the project?

Everett O'Keefe: Yeah, that's right. I took my buddy, Ed Rush, for his word.

Male Audience Member: I was in the interview where that's exactly what he did.

Mike Koenigs: I love that!

Everett O'Keefe: Yeah. I think, really honestly, it is all about execution. Whether you execute a podcast; books; anything that's going - you've just got to execute.

Mike Koenigs: That's great. All right, let's do the next one here.

Everett O'Keefe: So, we probably don't have time for all of these.

Mike Koenigs: You can just go through them real fast. So you met your next client, Blair at an event, you saw him at a hot seat.

Everett O'Keefe: All right. Blair, we met here. He approached John, actually, because we were on a marketing panel together on your stage and they hit it off. It turns out he had this great master plan and technique to save America a ton of money fixing our crumbling roadways. Amazing guy! And he likes to play rock guitar at his live events.

Mike Koenigs: And so, I'm going to just underscore this. The value of implementation, execution; one of our customers in the audience saw Everett and John on a panel talking and approached them. So again, there are people there who are like, "Hey, is there someone here who I can trust and I can work with?" And that's the kind of exposure you can get when we feature you on our stage; and again: everything we do, we do for a reason.

We've figured out a way to introduce people on the basis of trust and integrity and character and feelings. Again, it's the emotions that connect us and draw us together. And a logical mind will fall in place with the facts that we hear, but it starts there. So that's great, yeah.

Everett O'Keefe: And then Keppen Laszlo, a very successful businessman, actually approached me at an event because I'd been on a panel and he wanted to know more. He knew we had done several successful book launches and he wanted to do one with his book as well. So yeah, it kind of tumbled in. *The Resurrection Marriage*; a great guy, Ron McLain, is in my church in Fresno and saw what we had done with our own launch and with other people's launches and said, "I've got this idea for a book, I'd like to get it out. It has been on my heart and I know marriages need it," and we said, "Absolutely." And that's turned into follow-up projects; we just did a big video shoot for him for a high-end retreat as a result.

Mike Koenigs: Okay.

Everett O'Keefe: And then this story, some of you may have heard of it; do you want to go into it here?

Mike Koenigs: Yes!

Everett O'Keefe: Sure. Shane Randall from the community approached myself and also Victoria Greggs (who does a lot of Facebook stuff) and said, "Hey, I've got this megachurch, they've got a couple of projects. One is a pastor's book and one is a worship team CD." And we thought, "A CD? What do we do with a CD?" but we decided, "Why not use some of the same strategies we use for pushing a book to bestseller status for music?"

That is exactly what we ended up doing. We used the same Kindle launch strategy that we use for books; but we did it for CDs. We drove a ton of traffic to Amazon and iTunes. The church originally just wanted to do an iTunes promo because they figured everyone buys their stuff on iTunes and I held up my Android phone and I went, "I don't." I said, "From what I understand, there are some other people who own Android phones and maybe we have to do Amazon too." As a result, we actually ranked better in Amazon (where we were number 47 or 43 or something like that on all records on Amazon); because of that cross-platform of dominating Amazon and iTunes, it showed up on Billboard! That was not expected whatsoever.

Mike Koenigs: Wow! A top Billboard release!

Everett O'Keefe: But it was really because of coordinating with members of the community who have the appropriate specialties. Shane project-managed; he knew where to go, he had us do kind of the book launch-type stuff and the social media was handled by Victoria. Because of that coordination, it was a success. That's the same thing you can do, right?

Mike Koenigs: So Everett, we talked and we heard about this and said, "Okay. That's something we've never thought about because our best ideas come from the community that get shared." It's like someone either accidentally, or on purpose, used the tool in a different and unique way. We heard about the album launch and the book launch combined and we knew that that really connected to their hearts; and we said, "Hey, could you guys put together a webcast training inside the membership site for everyone else so they can see what you're doing?" They said, "Absolutely." Because again, they're not thinking, "How am I going to keep this for myself?" but instead, "How can I help other people along the way?" That's why Everett is here right now, because he's got a great abundance mindset.

So they did this presentation and I heard about it; after I saw it, I said, "Hey guys, why don't you stay on the line after this is done? I've got an idea for you." So they did; and I said, "You know you're sitting on a half-a-million to a two-million-dollar a year opportunity here? Think of all the mega churches and churches that are out there where the pastors have got a book idea; there's a choir that probably knows how to rock and roll and perform; and you guys could go and turn this into a real business."

There are other people who can model and replicate this; but also, what can this do to elevate their visibility and get some additional projects and jobs is pretty powerful.

Everett O'Keefe: Yeah. In fact, actually, in a very competitive category, we actually did the launch side of this, Zondervan Publishing, which is a division of, I think, Thomas Nelson. One of the giant companies actually was publishing this book, and we came on and did what we could to lift it.

That put it in a category we could never overtake, because some of the top books were ranked 140 or something in all of Amazon; that type of thing. But they got it to… I think it hit number 10, and was way over the top of some huge names in Christian marketing. I mean, anytime you're a Christian author and you can beat C.S. Lewis, you're doing pretty well. And they were elated, they really were elated. But really, all of this, Mike - and I know we're out of time but I will just tell you – do anything you can do to execute on the things that you're learning; you don't have to execute all of it. Execute some of it and see what happens with that.

The other thing is to latch onto the community. I mean, this has been huge. That has been absolutely pivotal in the success of our business… and honestly, latching onto the community was pivotal in the success of just me getting through the last several months. I had so many people reaching out and just saying, "Okay, I'm here. What can I do for you? How can I help you? What can I do to take some load off of what you're doing now that you've lost half of your ability to produce? You've lost your best friend." All of that; it has been astounding. It still comes back to this; it's an amazing place of tools, strategies and heart. It's really been an incredible time. And what is there but to be incredible going forward?

Mike Koenigs: I guess the last question is, what's next for you, your business and your family?

Everett O'Keefe: Well, kids tend to grow and they tend to start going to college and things like that. So we'll see how we float that boat with that going on. As far as our business goes; quite frankly, God has dropped an amazing guy in my lap who volunteers in our church's youth group and our high school group and happens to have learned how to use all of our equipment and learn Adobe Premiere - a month before John died. God just completely lined him up. His name is John Meyer and he has been an awesome help.

And I just know that things are going to continue to go really, really well. We've got a lot of business coming in; we continue to help people; and honestly, John Riding and I have all along felt that our job was being the expert; we're not interested in being the person on stage. We're not interested in being an author, really. I mean writing was just a proof of concept for us. We're interested in supporting others who have a message to get out.

There's a part in the Old Testament where armies are fighting and Moses is holding the staff of God up high... and as long as he can hold the staff up high, the army is winning, okay? But his arms are getting tired as the battle goes on through the day and he just can't hold it high... and then Aaron and Hur come up next to him and they each grab an arm and they hold Moses' arms up high. Then, the battle can be won. That's how we see ourselves, that's our role. We don't need to be Moses, I don't have a desire to be Moses. I do have a desire to hold Moses' arms up high. And so, that's what we do.

Interview #2: John Cote · How to Dominate a Market You Know Nothing About in Less Than Six Months

Mike Koenigs: We love to celebrate our customers' and clients' successes. John Cote has come a long way in a very short period of time and had some massive major breakthroughs in the past year. You've been part of the community for long?

John Cote: About five years.

Mike Koenigs: About five years. John is going to tell us his story in a moment, but I think what you're going to see are a couple of great examples that have to do with building momentum and creating luck for yourself. One of the big opportunities really came from how you named your book and how that's led into opportunity after opportunity after opportunity. So maybe before we get started with the Q&A and some of the slides that you've prepared, can you talk a little bit about who you are, where you came from? Maybe set us up with your back-story first?

John Cote: I'm a serial marketing buyer of stuff, which I stopped doing a long time ago when I met Mike. I've been using your systems for many years now. We started a local digital agency to help local businesses originally; just to do social media marketing. That's all we did. It was our niche. We were really good at it. Nobody else knew what was going on in that space in our area and we were crushing it. What we learned very quickly about a year later was that people competed and said, "Oh, I can do that too and I can do it for cheaper than John can do it." All of a sudden, it became a race to the bottom and I said, "Nope, I am not going there. I'm not going to do that." So we had to shift our focus and get ourselves in a place where we could go out and start doing consulting using the *Top Gun Consulting Toolkit* and your other systems.

So, in any case, our goal with this was to create a sustainable business that we could... that I didn't have to be out there doing it; doing it; doing it all day long. Because previously, I was the person; I was a solopreneur for the first couple of years and doing everything. How many of you have done that?

So in any case, we got to the point where Mike started talking about writing and publishing books. So I wrote *Mobilize Your Customers* and it became a #1 bestseller on Amazon, with Mike's help in a month using your systems. Go ahead and read the subtitle, Mike.

Mike Koenigs: *Create Powerful Word-of-Mouth Advertising Using Social Media, Video and Mobile Marketing to Attract New Customers and Skyrocket your Profits.*

John Cote: So about a year ago, I got a cold-call from a woman who runs the Medical Tourism Association conference that brings 2,500 attendees from 80 countries in Las Vegas. She said, "Hey, I was looking for a speaker online. I Googled word-of-mouth advertising and your book popped up, so I bought it, we read it and we want you to come speak at our event. Would you be interested?" And I said, "Sure, let me send you a speaker contract over with my fees," and she said, "Well, that's the hook; because it's a medical conference, you have to do it for free. You have to pay all of your expenses. We're not going to get you hotel room, nothing; you have to pay for everything." And I said, "Tell me a little bit more about it." She told me about all these attendees. I said, "Great! I'll be there!" There were authors who were *New York Times'* bestsellers and lots of highly qualified people who could become clients of mine."

Mike Koenigs: So just to be clear, John got asked to speak on the stage and there were *New York Times* bestsellers there, so it elevated his value. That was part of the big opportunity. John suddenly grew his credibility.

John Cote: Absolutely. So, I show up there and I had set up a Crowd Grabber campaign so that we could capture attendee information and we did the whole pitch from stage and it was great. While we were up there, I did two very important things. So I had been on stage with Mike that fall; right before I went, he said, "Hey, give away free copies of your book." So I had like 250 copies of the book, dropped-shipped from Amazon directly to the hotel. They trucked them up to the room for me and my lovely and talented wife Jennifer helped me to pass them out while I was doing my presentation. We handed them out and built a list.

What was really cool was it was the last presentation of the day and it was happy hour down on the trade show floor right after that. So everyone went, and they scattered and I was like, "Oh man, I think I might have just lost my opportunity." So I went down to the tradeshow floor with a bunch of these books in my hand and as soon as I walk in the door, I had people, "Oh wow! John, I loved your speech, can I have your autograph?" I said, "Okay, sure." So I started signing books. All of a sudden, people started coming around and saying, "Well, who is this guy and what's going on? Can I have one of those?" So I started giving away copies of the books and my business cards. It was a really big hit. The organization invited me back this year!

The big thing that happened there is that I challenged everyone and said, "Look, podcasting is one of the things that we've just been talking about. It's really blowing up. You should really go out and start a podcast on medical tourism; all of you should; because when you go to iTunes and you type in "medical tourism," nothing comes up. There is no competition. You could totally own the niche." And everyone was like, "Whoa! That's great," and they gave me a big round of applause… and then nobody did anything.

So in two months later in January (I presented November of last year), I started thinking about podcasting in the medical tourism industry. I said to myself, "I need to do something with this because this is a massive opportunity. It's a multibillion dollar industry that's very fractured; there's no real leader in this entire industry." And I saw an interview with you and John Lee Dumas from *Entrepreneur On Fire*, who talked about how he had created his podcast and I said, "I can do this. I can totally do this." I'm not an expert on medical tourism. I'm not a medical expert, none of that. But now after doing 75 podcast episodes with people from all over the world who are patients, doctors, surgeons, medical experts and basically talked with all these people; and all I did was to ask them to tell me their story. Share their pain point with me, what their problem was, and how they were able to travel to another country, in most cases, and get successful, affordable, world-class medical care. Now I've become an authority on the topic and the biggest players in the industry all know who I am!

So the first problem is defining what medical tourism is; and I had a passion for it because my lovely wife, Jennifer, is a two-time cancer survivor. She traveled, like Mike did, to Duke University many years ago to get treatment for her cancer. So this was a big thing for me; I was really interested in the technology of it and what was going on. So I had a passion for it in the first place, but I knew nothing about it. So I said, "I'm not going to let that stop me." I set a goal: April 21st, I will launch. I had 10 weeks and I did it. And it was a daily podcast; a daily show to start with.

So anyway, what happened is we took the top 20 most popular episodes from that podcast, transcribed and edited them and made a book out of them. Now that I'm a leader in the industry in less than a year, am speaking at the next event AND I'll have my new book that will be a #1 bestseller – I'll be back as an industry expert!

I'm speaking again at the same conference in Washington D.C. I'm bringing another 200 books, giving them out. We've got appointments out all over the place, so it's been great. So it's all kind of come full circle and around now at this point.

Mike Koenigs: This is great. One of the strategies we teach in the Publish and Profit system are stage techniques; how to use the stage to capture leads, and what John did was really great.

You differentiated yourself with the book. It was the title, or a couple of characters in the subtitle. That's why it's so important to have an SEO-enhanced subtitle (Search Engine Optimized) that's very meaningful to an audience with a pain and with an outcome in mind. How do you use 'blank' to get 'blank', right? That's a very powerful formula. Someone finds your book, buys it, reads it, calls you up and says, "John, we want you to be there." You speak and you took the risk, all on your own dime.

You were able to buy your own books in bulk from Amazon, delivered right to the hotel for about $2.00 each. Then from stage, you give away your book and use the Crowd Grabber to capture leads. Now you've built a list and are seen as a niche celebrity.

From there, how many customers or prospects walked up to you and said, "John, I love what you talk about, will you do 'blank' for me? Will you do mobile or video marketing or help me market my medical tourism business or my hospital?"

Have you gotten direct business out of it so far?

John Cote: Yeah, absolutely. So we had people approach us right away who came to us and they were from multiple countries. It was interesting. I never intended to be an international businessperson but this opportunity landed in my lap and I took it. So we've got to the point where the biggest thing I've had to realize is that people in other countries (even though I've travelled extensively around the world), they do business very, very differently. So the sales process is much, much longer than I was expecting.

Actually, someone in this room who I have talked with before told me, "Be patient." He had dealt an international business before and said, "It may take you six months through a year to close some of these deals." Every month, get a call from some of these companies saying, "We still want to work with you. We haven't allocated our dollars anywhere else. We're going to go ahead and do business with you. It's just that we have a board of directors and this and that and different departments. It just takes time."

So this is a long play for us. We are really in this for the long haul. So, of the ones that we spoke to, we had about a dozen, really solid contacts and leads from Thailand, a couple in India, down in Costa Rica, Mexico, and the Bahamas and over in France; and five or six of those companies are still actively talking with us right now and want to do deals with us. Of those or in addition to those, since we launched the podcast, we've had other people immediately contact us and say, "We want to sponsor your show." I was turning money down four months ago when we launched and people were like, "What are you nuts?" One of my Mastermind partners is sitting in this room and he's like, "Dude, you're nuts. Take the money." And I said, "I understand where you're coming from, but I don't know what I have yet." I had no idea what kind of numbers we were going to get. We'll get into all that in a minute.

But the point for me was I wanted to make sure I was providing value for the listeners and that I was creating great content, great stories and making sure that whoever I do partner with, they're getting value, and they're getting people coming to them that are going to want to do business with them, and they will know they can trust me through the content that they're getting out of our show. So we have waited to do that and because this conference happens to be coming up next month, we decided, "Hey, we'll start; we'll meet with you in person at the conference." So we have six solid set up appointments and we told them, "Look, I've got two sets of ad spots available, 15-second pre-roll and a 30 mid-roll and so that's it. So there are six of you that are interested so bring your wallets; it's going to be expensive and it's not just about the money, it's about being the best fit. So I want you to come and tell me why I should work with you because I want to give the best service that I can to our listeners out there."

Mike Koenigs: That is great. Let's show a couple of the slides, because you've got some proof about what's been going on. Just go ahead and click on the green button.

John Cote: Yeah. So, the podcasting thing; I got asked right after we launched to be on the cover of *Podcasting Magazine*. That's Drew Griffin, one of our fellow community members right here. I was very honored to be there and I got some traffic off of that which was great. We recently moved into new offices up on the top floor of a really nice building. We're on the right side. We actually have a little patio out there; though we don't get to see the ocean like you do here in San Diego. This is over in Hanceville, Alabama, but we could set up a space where we've got a studio and I've got a green screen, so I can do kind of the bookshelf concept there and I can also set up that TV. I usually turn it around and have it facing me so that I can do live broadcast with Mike and with other people and kind of do the live webcast and things like that.

We also have a green screen studio. We have a couch-and-chair kind of studio. So we looked at what Mike had done and I've been to your studios and had decided that, "Yeah, I want to mirror that," and let's not reinvent the wheel. Let's just set three or four studios up that we can use. We've already had clients locally say, "Yeah, we'd like to come and lease your space to do video work in there." So that's been a great result.

Next, I needed to build an audience for my podcast. I hired a professional, another person from our Publish and Profit Community here who was really good at Facebook ads, and I told her, "Look, I want you to find me people who have traveled for or are interested in medical tourism in some way; whether they're professionals or just someone who wants to travel."

We went from 0 to 3,700 likes in a span of about two-and-a-half weeks right up to the launch and we had a whole process going out. We had a bunch of people talking about the page. And on day one of the launch, we were #1 in our respective category in medicine; and then, within a week, we were #1 in health, which is one of the major categories on iTunes... all because of the strategies that we've learned from the Publish and Profit System. So I just took the screenshot yesterday. We had 285,000 download in four months. I'm not exactly sure how that happened, honestly. But the bottom line is, the strategies that I learned here allowed me to go out and get that kind of success which has been attracting the interest from sponsors and potential customers.

Mike Koenigs: So that's about 3,500 new downloads per day right now.

John Cote: Everyday. That's right, everyday. So you could see there are some of the proof screen shots there: top podcast #1 over there, debuted number on launch day in the medicine category. If you typed in "medical tourism podcast" into Google, our stuff popped up before we even launched the show. I hadn't even launched the show yet. I did a cool little promotional video and put it out there a couple of weeks before the show, and we were already popping up at #1. If you typed in my name or medical tourism or anything like that into iTunes, all of our stuff shows up. All of our episodes show up.

It's a huge deal for SEO. So now you can just tell people when they meet you, "I don't carry cards anymore." They say, "Well, how can I get a hold of you?" And I say, "Either give me your name and number, or type my name into Amazon, type my name into iTunes"… and it's all the social proof that I need for them to say, "Wow! Who is this guy? I want to work with him!"

Mike Koenigs: Yeah, you own it.

John Cote: Yeah, I totally own that space. So there is the *Podcasting Magazine* cover. [John shows a picture of him on the cover of a magazine].

Mike Koenigs: Great! So to summarize, John wrote a book, someone found the book and called you up and gave you this speaking opportunity. You saw an opportunity to own a niche by creating a podcast in a market you knew nothing about. Now what John is able to get just about anyone in that business to agree to be interviewed by him. Now he's building momentum and create a whole bunch of value that will be extremely valuable to his target audiences - which are medical tourism doctors and hospitals. Then they can either say, "John, I'd like to hire you to provide marketing services for my business," or "We'd like to become a sponsor or advertiser on the show." At this point - with almost 300,000 total downloads, right?

John Cote: Yeah.

Mike Koenigs: John is in a strong position to command significant advertising dollars. But imagine this: after every interview he is doing (interviewing, of course, with people who have gone and done medical tourism; but now he can also interview professionals at the hospitals), John can call up anyone and say, "Hey, I'd like to interview you on my show and feature your hospital or feature your services." Who's going to say no to that, right?

John Cote: Yeah.

Mike Koenigs: More importantly, when he is done, he can use those magical words, "I have an idea about how you can grow your business." Bam! Now, they're in a spot saying, "Yes, what can you do with us or for us?" And you can say, "Well, I'm very selective about who I work with." So now I can push them away and they have to actually fight to work with them; a complete power reversal. It's a very powerful position to be in. Instead of going out and begging clients to work with John, the prospects come to John and beg for him to interview or work with them!

John Cote: And I've actually had that very conversation. About half of our shows, we really try and focus on the patient. It's a very patient-oriented podcast. As a matter of fact, Karol is sitting here in the front row. She and her husband Dr. Thomas Clark have a weight loss surgery center, and I reached out to them and said, "Hey, I'd love to interview you guys," because what they're doing is very, very cool and interesting and we should talk more about it with their patients. I interviewed them and one of their patients, they were gracious enough to bring me in their offices, and they're included in the new book, "Healthcare Elsewhere" because of the cool stuff that they're doing with their practice... I have told that to other organizations around the world and they're like, "Wait, they're doing what? Can you help us with something like that?" My reply is, "Absolutely."

And so, they're calling me, asking me for the interview. We do the interview and at the end of the interview, I say, "Hey, you know what? I'm just curious, how are you advertising? How are you targeting North American patients? Who is your perfect client?" One thing I'd really like to point out, and we're doing something that's a little bit different here, is that this show is not for medical tourism professionals per se, it's for people who are interested in learning more about changing their life. They've got a medical problem that they can't solve because their insurance doesn't cover it or stem cells aren't allowed here in the United States or it's too expensive and they can get world-class health care traveling to another place. We tell that story and they're interested in hearing from the experts, but nobody on that show has ever heard me say anything about "marketing agencies" or "I've got this product". I'm not selling them anything. I am trying to provide great content for these people so they will come back to the show and share the show with other people. And what has happened is a natural extension of that which was our intent; people who are professionals in the industry who are coming to us and seeing us as the experts and saying, "You have the world's leading medical tourism podcast. How did you do that? Can you help us?"

So we're getting clients even though that's not who I was targeting with the show. So think outside of the box a little bit. I try and think of different ways that you might be able to reach people in different ways with a show.

Mike Koenigs: Very good. I could interview you for another hour and a half but I'd like you to complete this sentence: "Because of my book…"

John Cote: Yeah.

Mike Koenigs: So if you're going to give us three giant "because of my book," what are three big things that have occurred because of your book? And we didn't even talk about your other book, which is about real estate marketing on Facebook. So John didn't know anything about either real estate marketing or really Facebook. He found someone who was an expert in that and co-authored a book; now he's an expert, an authority. He's got his name associated with it, which helps him also pick up some more projects and clients. But because of your book… what?

John Cote: Because of my book, we have a great new studio and a lot of potential new clients in an international industry that has literally unlimited potential.

Because of my book, it has gotten me onto the stage at worldwide, world-class events with *New York Times* bestselling authors that I get to rub elbows with and talk with. Some of them are coming to me and asking me, "How did you do that?" Because they were giving away one book and I gave away 200, and because of my book - or actually, because of my podcast - I have this book and it's not in just one format. All of these things together have put me into a lead where literally I can make a phone call to an industry expert like Mike Koenigs or John Lee Dumas or any big industry guru. If I've got a problem or a situation that I don't have a solution for, I'm on their radar to the point now where I can call them and ask for help and hire them directly if I need help for a larger client because it's something that I'm not an expert in. I don't need to be the expert anymore. I can outsource the rest of the stuff.

Mike Koenigs: All right, very nice.

The whole idea behind **Publish and Profit** is it starts out with your idea. It's publishing in multiple formats. It's promoting in different formats. So you can be seen, heard, viewed anytime, anywhere on any device. And you think about how every format, every distribution mechanism builds on and builds momentum. These are multi pliers. They're force multipliers.

Let's give John a big congratulations on his success, very nice!

EVERY STRATEGY IN THIS INTERVIEW STEP-BY-STEP

Everything discussed in this interview is taught inside the Publish and Profit system. And if you don't want to do it yourself, there are certified coaches and consultants in the community you can hire to do it for you.

Visit www.PublishAndProfit.com/BookBonus
or text your email address to (858) 707-7417
for details on how you can get started.

Interview #3: Karol Clark - How to Sell to Your Competitors and Make an Extra $150,000 in a Year

Mike Koenigs: This is a really great success story. Karol Clark has been in our community since 2012. Karol, will you tell everyone a little bit about your backstory; where you live, where you're from, what you do, and what's been going on in your business?

Karol Clark: I live in Newport News, Virginia, with my very modest husband, Dr. Thomas Clark and our four children. We have a practice called "Center for Weight Loss Success". We provide surgical services for people to lose weight, as well as non-surgical services, fitness and nutrition all under one roof. This has been a concept that we had been working towards as a dream.

For a long time, we had a separate surgical practice and a medical practice and we decided in 2011 that we would combine those under one roof when we built a 10,000-square-foot facility. We did this with the idea that people would come into a very warm and inviting atmosphere and we would provide them with concierge services so they would feel comfortable and safe and see success... and we see that success every day. It's really very, very rewarding.

We can help a lot of people without any surgery with our systems. But for some people, that isn't enough.

For people who are having weight loss surgery, we're not only concerned with the surgery itself, but what's most important is the follow-up process. So for that whole first year, they're going through drastic changes. That's the time when you really need to engage with them and help them understand that they have a new tool to lose weight... but it's not a magic bullet; it's just a tool.

Education is really important - which is not something that's commonly provided in many surgical offices. But for us, it's the right thing to do. It's not anywhere where you make any money but it's the right thing to do and that's where you see these awesome success stories. We probably have a waiting list for success stories and we really enjoy it.

We built this big facility. It's about 10,000-square-feet; we paid attention to every detail in there. And you figure, "if you build it, they will come."

Mike Koenigs: That never works though, does it? Behind every successful business is great marketing.

Karol Clark: My husband is arguably (he's very modest, but arguably), the most experienced practicing bariatric surgeon in the US, having done more than 4,000 weight loss procedures. So you'd think, "Oh, he'll have a huge following and customers will just come out of the woodwork and rush towards us." But when we combined two offices and changed the name, branding was an issue. And to compound that, people weren't really sure what happened with both practices and we had a couple of things going on in the community where a couple of competitors created some rumors that we weren't in practice anymore; some things that were really detrimental.

So we've built this huge facility and it was awesome, it was everything we ever dreamed of. And we have patients coming through, of course, and patient referrals. But our numbers went down.

Mike Koenigs: So you guys were losing money?

Karol Clark: Yes, and it was scary; it was really scary. It was one of those times and we had this awesome staff, you can see them up there. [Shows pictures of her team]

Mike Koenigs: Oh, yeah. There they are.

Karol Clark: The staff is like family to us. We love them. They're just very passionate. They believe the same things we believe. They're like family, and they rely on us; so if anyone has been through that - some sleepless nights, that sort of thing - it's us. Because during that rough time, we were afraid we got in over our heads and would have to reduce our staff.

And so, I was introduced in 2012 to Mike Koenigs and his products and the awesome team and the systems that are built here. His marketing really spoke to me; I came to a few events and it's never really been the same since. I just learned what he taught, what the team taught, caught on to the energy, met phenomenal people who have provided opportunities all the way and took whatever I learned and just applied it. It didn't happen overnight, but it's been a pretty cool ride.

Mike Koenigs: All right. So I'm going to ask you a couple of questions.

Karol Clark: Sure.

Mike Koenigs: The first one is, before we get into the solution, I'm going to ask you just how bad things got. Obviously, I just saw you had an emotional reaction, so how scary and what was like, the worst situation? Where did it get the scariest?

Karol Clark: Well, I have to tell you. In the healthcare profession, it's very precarious right now, which everyone can probably identify with. But back then; almost every physician was being bought up by health systems. So to remain independent and to stay true to your promise, it's an anomaly. In fact, in the whole State of Virginia, Tom is the only one not owned by a huge health system.

That spoke to our purpose and our passion and what we really wanted to accomplish and we could have easily sold out. We had hospitals coming in and saying, "We want to buy your practice. You're the most experienced guy in town. You've built all this stuff." That's not what we wanted. We wanted to be in control. We wanted to control our destiny and to see and to do things in a very unique concierge style.

Mike Koenigs: But how bad did things get?

Karol Clark: Oh, golly! I don't like to admit failure, ever.

Mike Koenigs: I know. That's why I'm asking you that question.

Karol Clark: I know.

Mike Koenigs: I'm not going to let you go down another rabbit hole one more time. So how bad did things get? What was the worst before you had your breakthrough?

Karol Clark: When we were under construction, for nine months, we didn't take a paycheck. That was because we did that consciously. We had saved up for it. We took all of our money and put it into the building; we put it into our dream. But with four kids and what we had going on, that wasn't easy. So it was one of those things where there was a period of time where - I'm one of those people - it kept me up at night.

Mike Koenigs: So you got that precarious with your staff too? You didn't have any big worries?

Karol Clark: No, I would never. I was transparent to them and I would never... no, they were always taken care of. The bank was always taken care of and the insurance was always taken care of. It was just our home life that was not as taken care of, which is the scary thing.

Mike Koenigs: Right, I got it; "entrepreneurial disease."

Karol Clark: Yeah, it is.

Mike Koenigs: All right.

Karol Clark: But that was important to us, to take care of them; and to this day, some of them have been with us for 20 years and they're awesome. That was pretty transparent. But anyhow, it got to be at that point.

Mike Koenigs: So the bottom line is, you don't take a paycheck for nine months. You open up this place; there's brand confusion. It sounds like some competitors were creating at least the appearance that maybe you guys weren't in business anymore, that kind of thing.

Karol Clark: Right. And I don't like to focus on the negative, but we had some of that negativity going on.

Mike Koenigs: That's all right. It is what it is, right?

Karol Clark: It was reality, yeah.

Mike Koenigs: This is an entrepreneur's circumstance.

Karol Clark: Yeah. I don't think I've ever verbally said any of that in front of a group.

Mike Koenigs: How does it feel?

Karol Clark: It feels good now, today.

Mike Koenigs: Yeah, exactly. It's always fun to talk about the way things used to be, right?

Karol Clark: Yeah, like afterwards.

Mike Koenigs: Yeah, after it's done.

Karol Clark: We had gone from a seven-figure business. It was just one of those things, you were there... and then you weren't so much. But it feels okay today.

Mike Koenigs: Thank you for your transparency and vulnerability. I think the first thing that I'd like to show off here are your three books. From the time you got exposed to our systems; how long did it take for you from when you decided to write book #1 until it was done? And then let's go through the three books and specifically what they did for your business each time.

Karol Clark: Sure. The first one that we did was *Is Weight Loss Surgery Right for You?* That's our bread and butter. That's the one I wanted to get out there. We do a lot of education so it had a ton of content. We put it all together, I started the book after I went through your training in November and released it in April.

Karol Clark: I probably could have done it sooner. I sort of had anxiety over the whole process. But once I did it, then there was no stopping.

So we did this book, and I'm going to talk a little bit about it and some future slides. But the biggest thing that it did for us was it increased our awareness of our practice and it also differentiated us when people came in and were considering various surgeons for who they wanted to select for their surgery.

Mike Koenigs: So you can I say "I wrote the book on..."

Karol Clark: Right. And I'm a number-one Amazon best-selling author, and that attracted more clients as well.

Mike Koenigs: Okay. Just getting it on Amazon, did it attract clients outside of your local area?

Karol Clark: Not immediately.

Mike Koenigs: Okay. I guess we'll get to that a little bit later. Then when you wrote the second book.

Karol Clark: This is another one related to surgery. We do a very thorough pre-operative class and there's a lot of places we have patients coming in who had surgery elsewhere and they said, "Nobody ever even sat down with me before surgery. I had no idea what I was getting into. I had no idea what I could experience." And so, we took all of our education materials and put it into a book that we could share, so that other people who were having surgery elsewhere could still have the education that they needed.

Mike Koenigs: So it was really how to do business with you; what to expect; so that you don't have to repeat yourself over and over.

Karol Clark: Correct.

Mike Koenigs: But packaged in such a way that it legitimized you further.

Karol Clark: Right.

Mike Koenigs: Okay. How long did this take to write from start to finish?

Karol Clark: This one? Well, when I write, I like to go to a place called Lake Gaston in North Carolina. I just go there for a period of time. It took me about three days to take it and put it all together and it was ready to go and be formatted and it was ready to roll. I did both of them [shows the 2nd and 3rd books]. This one I did in probably two days, this one probably in about three days. Each time, it takes about two to three days for me.

We do the outline together, Tom and I; we gather up the content that we've already created. And then I like to just go and knock it out.

Mike Koenigs: So it's basically repurposed content; in this case, a combination of marketing, legitimacy, case studies, interviews and stories.

Karol Clark: Right. And in each one, we followed your model exactly. We had a lead capture that was included in each one. I created videos so every one of them has the 20 videos already created within the membership site. So everybody who obtains the book then can go ahead and obtain the free videos that go along with it. And that's a lead for us that we can then follow up with to come to the clinic.

Mike Koenigs: So the opportunity to opt in after getting a lot of information this way is by saying something like, "Hey, if you'd like to watch the videos, sign up here." That way, you indoctrinate the reader with either the book or videos. Do you send out one video a day or do they have access to all the videos right away when they register?

Karol Clark: We actually gave them access to all of them at the same time.

We deliver all the content from inside a membership site. They're also getting emails with upsells and really building more trust and explaining what they're getting with each video… and then also adding how to reach us for more information or upsells for any other services they may want to purchase.

And then the last one we did was one on medical and non-surgical weight loss. That's the red one.

We made the books as a series, and we have a retail store at the clinic. So we have this in the retail store as well as on Amazon.

Mike Koenigs: So you have people buying your marketing materials cleverly disguised as book, isn't that nice?

Karol Clark: It is!

Mike Koenigs: Okay. So if we move forward, we've got a couple of things. The first one, I think that's pretty obvious. Can you talk about how this generated leads for you outside of the onsite store in your clinic? You said earlier that you didn't start getting people from Amazon to you right away.

Karol Clark: Right.

Mike Koenigs: But when did you start seeing this? Obviously, you put this together. But where did you start seeing some initial response? Again, I think what I want to drive towards is, for every lead that you got as a result of the book, where did they come from? How long did it take to go through essentially your sale cycle or your indoctrination cycle? And if you got, let's say, 100 people who had your book, how many people would actually interact with you and potentially become a customer at that point?

Karol Clark: Sure. Out of the three books, we ended up with about 270 very qualified leads. And because we provided them with the video content at one time, we would actually see sales conversions where it was pretty quick for them to then want some services.

Mike Koenigs: "Pretty quick"... meaning: days, weeks, months?

Karol Clark: Within days. Most people who want weight loss; they're an interesting bunch. 70% of the population has a BMI of 30 or more so they're considered obese... and they are researching information all the time. The important thing is to be in front of them when they're ready to buy and to show social proof that what you're offering really works. For us, it's a long-term solution; not a quick fix... although we do have two-week programs.

And what happened most often was, the surgical clients ended up coming in for a seminar. They're preparing for weight loss surgery, really, a lot those people, they already had surgery or they were already slated to have surgery with either us or another surgeon.

Mike Koenigs: So it really went from book to seminar to patient. But did you have some people bypass that set and say, "Look, I'm ready to come in and travel too from another part of the country or world for my surgery?"

Karol Clark: We did.

Mike Koenigs: So getting back to the numbers. If I were watching you right now I'd say, "All right, so you sell 270 books. How many customers do you figure you've got as a result of that?"

Karol Clark: We easily had just over 100. And I'm not talking all for surgery. Some of them ended up just purchasing non-surgical two-week jump-start programs where they wanted to lose 5 to 25 pounds in two weeks. Some of them may have seen our product and they lived locally and they came into our store just to see what we had to offer. We have a couple of other programs, like a metabolism check-up where you get some lab work and you meet with the physician; it's a shorter program. So if I gather together all of those together... well over a hundred.

Mike Koenigs: So if you're going to guess - just in terms of what the sales value of those 270 books were... just again, I'm just asking for a guess.

Karol Clark: I would probably say a couple of hundred thousand.

Mike Koenigs: Okay. That's not too bad for a book.

Karol Clark: No. And a lot of these people, once they're clients of ours, they're patients for life; so they represent ongoing recurring revenue.

Mike Koenigs: Fantastic. So your seven-figure business increased by another $145,000?

Karol Clark: It was more. I'd say another couple of hundred, but what you see here is very uncommon; because the area of bariatric surgery - fewer insurance companies are covering it; a large portion of the population are candidates but those who actually follow through is less than 1%. So you're seeing a lot of economic impact and our competitors were all losing market shares and were having less surgeries; whereas our sales are actually going up. For a seven-figure business, you may be like, "Well, what's $145,000?" It's big when you think that your competitors are losing their market share and they're experiencing less revenue, we're way ahead of the game.

Mike Koenigs: That's great. Here we go, seminar to surgery conversion rates. [shows a graph indicating their sales are climbing]

Karol Clark: This is the biggest takeaway point for us. What happens is, if you're considering weight loss surgery, we require everyone does either a webinar or comes in for a seminar. So the book *Preparing for Weight Loss Surgery*... what we do now is, as they come in for their seminar, they actually leave with a book in hand, so that they have all of our information right in their hands, and then we're at the forefront of their minds; because they're researching different physicians, but we're ahead.

For example, last Saturday we had a seminar and we had people come in. We had one woman come in and said, "I'm not planning on having surgery here, I just came to get the information." She got the book, she came out and said "Sign me up." It's the presentation as well from Tom and the whole office environment. She came out and said, "Give me my book and sign me up for my one-on-one consultation, I'm staying." This happens all the time with the book.

Mike Koenigs: That's fantastic!

Karol Clark: And that's probably one of the biggest things; we just give them away to people considering surgery and it's really cheap for us.

Self-pay surgery cases; this is a niche that we go after for a couple of reasons. When people want to pay for surgery, first, they don't think they can afford it; so we've negotiated probably the lowest price in most of the United States for people to have surgery which includes everything; hospital, physician and anesthesia. This is a big market that we're going after because we provide the concierge services and we also have this full follow-up program for a whole year and that's included in the program.

For people who are paying, they want two things. They want the experience and they want exclusivity. So they get the experience with the most experienced surgeon and they also get exclusivity with this one-year program that ensures a much higher likelihood of long-term success.

Mike Koenigs: So you've got compliance built in. So you really took the book and then turned the it into the "what" and the "how" is not just your surgery, but other services and even information products you sell, right?

Karol Clark: Right.

Mike Koenigs: So you've essentially created an information product that could stand on its own as well. Is that right?

Karol Clark: Right. We actually have four informational products now. One is "Weight Management University for Weight Loss Surgery". That's where everyone's included. It's a full one-year program with a membership site and a hard copy that's mailed to them once a month to tell them what to expect this month; what to expect next month; recipes; success stories; additional information about weight loss. We have a Weight Management University, which is a typical six-month program we use mostly onsite.

In January I happened to have some surgery; so I took that time to write our next product which is my Weight Loss Academy, that also includes a 21-day jump-start. And that's a program that's a digital program at the moment, and it's something that physicians can incorporate into their practice so they can actually provide weight loss services to their clients - as hands-on or hands-off as they want.

They can just refer people there and receive some referral revenue back; or I can teach them how to incorporate it into their practice and tell them exactly what they need to counsel on at every visit; and they can get an office visit for it as well.

Mike Koenigs: That's great. So you've really got inspiration and motivation and compliance built into the process.

Karol Clark: Right.

Mike Koenigs: So, opportunities. You've have a speaking opportunity that popped up… or a couple of them?

Karol Clark: Right. Tom, he speaks at ASBP which is the American Society for Bariatric Physicians. He's the surgeon representative and they want to add him to their board. But he does this two times a year which are national conferences, and they also have him doing webinar training for their members once a quarter.

With podcasts, John Cote mentioned we were on their "Healthcare Elsewhere" podcast, which has been phenomenal for generating leads. He's also been great in terms of making connections for us so we can attract more of the clientele that really want to pay for services but are having trouble finding an affordable and a comprehensive opportunity for them. So he's been great and a huge help. I did another podcast with another community member, Steve. People within the Publish and Profit community find out what you're doing and you can share your success and you can promote each other.

Mike Koenigs: That's great. So that's inside our community.

Karol Clark: Right. And then also, I did a couple of things in Canada and multiple things locally for organizations around us.

Mike Koenigs: Obviously, some of that is happening inside of our community. But speaking opportunities are happening because of the books?

Karol Clark: Absolutely, but because of your tools as well. All of those videos all went out and were automated and sent everywhere to increase a ubiquity footprint; and then we also sent out press releases and followed everything sort of to a tee; or at least tried to.

Mike Koenigs: You talked about medical tourism. The exposure from the podcasts; you've actually seen customers come to you or is it because of the books? Is the podcast too early to produce results at this point?

Karol Clark: The podcast has increased our exposure and it has actually increased our opportunities with other people who are facilitating medical tourism.

Mike Koenigs: So referrals really work.

Karol Clark: I haven't really seen the full impact from that, but we're working on a number of different things and I see that that will happen.

And I think it all layers on top of each other. We even just had a client now from Nigeria, she's doing awesome. I can't wait to get her to a point where she's comfortable having an interview with us. But she's doing phenomenal; and so, we're starting to attract international clients and people from elsewhere within the Unites States who value that experience in something that's affordable, where they don't have to actually leave the Unites States for surgery.

Mike Koenigs: That's right. And then you're actually starting to package, essentially, and license your content and your products to other weight loss surgeons, which is a big leap for a lot of people. The standard way is, "Well, how would I sell my competitive advantage to other people?"

Karol Clark: Right.

Mike Koenigs: So talk a little bit about that and how that's working out for you. You're basically a consultant to your husband and to other people in the industry now.

Karol Clark: Right, right. Well, the next time I'm going to talk to you I'll probably have more outcomes from that. I just launched Weight Loss Practice Builder. I had to spend some time building all the marketing funnels and an affiliate program that is incorporated into that. So that's all ready to roll. I've talked with a Canadian group; I've talked to some people out in Oregon; so I've got some feelers out there, things are in the works.

Surgeons are a little bit of a different animal because they like to do the surgery, they don't care about the follow-up as much. It's not that they don't care, but that's not where they want to spend their energy; and a lot of times they don't want to take information from another surgeon. But that's all starting to come along as well. I think they realize their patients need it and this is a really simple way for them to white-label our system and get their name in front of their patient every single month and increase their referrals.

Mike Koenigs: So really, the compliance and the retention ends up being a service to them, and ultimately, to you.

I know you've got more books and products this coming year. When you look at what you've done and where you are right now, what is next? Where do you see your business heading, if you're going to give us the 30-second snapshot? Maybe there's a better way to ask this; here's what I'd like to say: if you knew now what you knew then after the past couple of years developing and doing the books and the products, if you were going to shorten the cycle and let's say you're going to get the same results in, say, six months, what would you do and what would your advice be to someone else? Because someone might be sitting here saying, "Well, I don't have a weight loss clinic," and be saying "This doesn't apply"; but the fact is, all businesses are the same. So when you think about how other people can apply the knowledge, the wisdom and experience that you've built up and compress it, four-to-one for example, or five-to-one, what advice would you have?

Karol Clark: I would say you need to take time to think about what it is that you're offering and what business model you want to set up. I spend a lot of time thinking that through and I almost believe in making sure everything is totally perfect before I launch something, because I would never want to have someone dissatisfied. I would say figure it out and then just go do it.

The first one took me so much longer because I was like "How do I do this? I don't know. Is it enough information? Is it good information? Are people going to read it?" And it was like, throw that out the window and just go for it!

Mike Koenigs: Good enough?

Karol Clark: You want a quality product, yeah. But I was going for perfection, and yeah, right; the other thing is, know your avatar. Know who it is that you're going to market your product to, because it does no good to create this great beautiful product if...

Mike Koenigs: Oh!

Karol Clark: Yeah, if you've totally missed the boat on who you're going to sell it to.

Mike Koenigs: Write to your best friend, the person who needs it the most, right?

Karol Clark: Right, exactly. And feel good about it.

Mike Koenigs: So here's the last question. We've got our "because of my book...." thing going on with the other interviews. So I'd like to hear three "because of my books" from you. What do you think the three greatest transformations have been for you personally; for your family and your husband and your married life, your connection with him; and then the business and/or the people you serve?

What are your "because of my books" that you look back and say, "A couple of years have gone by..." What are the biggest "ahas" and the greatest feel-goods for you?

Karol Clark: The biggest one is, personally, it's the people coming up and saying, "Your book made a huge difference for me. I didn't get this information; I didn't have the access to this information; and now I have it. It makes total sense and it really changed how I was utilizing my new tool or my contemplation of having surgery." So having people say that the book really changed their lives, it's amazing.

Mike Koenigs: Have you had anyone say, "Your book saved my life! If I hadn't read it, I wouldn't have done..." something?

Karol Clark: Right. Every day, at least for people who have surgery, they come in, and it's a very happy place to work. People are excited. They get to their hundred pounds or however much they're losing. They are excited. We have a wet eye in the house all the time. That's really the most rewarding. And knowing that we stayed true to our purpose and we didn't sell out; because that would have been an easy way out, but it would have been a very frustrating thing. And I know that for my husband and me is would be very hard to live with everyday; knowing that you're being dictated to and forced to do things in a certain traditional way and not doing what's right for your clients.

Mike Koenigs: So you've got freedom and you're doing business on your terms, even though everyone else sold out.

Karol Clark: Yeah, right. That was probably one of them. The other one is the connections. The connections with this community and just with people that you meet from having your information out there is amazing. It can catapult you and your business to eternity and beyond, I guess; but the places you never thought you'd be or go. I think that's probably a pretty cool thing as well.

And then the next thing is, because of the book, it gave me the confidence to branch out and actually develop a whole new practice, Weight Loss Practice Builder, and really take that and help other physicians who are out there right now saying, "I don't like my job. I'm so frustrated. I'm seeing a hundred patients a day." They're not enjoying it. It's a very difficult environment to be in and it's frustrating to see, because you know they're good people and they got into the profession for good reasons. So to help them help their patients more, and then also experience a healthier bottom line as a result of it... hopeful, healthier living, that's what I'm looking forward to.

Karol Clark: Without the book, I don't think I would have had the confidence or the ability to move in that direction; along with recommendations from you, your team and members in the community that support along the way. So those are my biggest takeaways, "because of my book."

Mike Koenigs: Congratulations. So, the last question: is it easy, does it work and can anyone do it knowing what you know now and what you see?

Karol Clark: I'm a clinician. I love computers; I love marketing; I love all that. But I don't have any formal training writing books; and I found it to be extremely easy, with plenty of support; and if you have a question, somebody is there to help you through it. It's a turnkey system. I know that's probably a cliché sort of a word, but it truly is. If you just follow what you're taught, really, you can't fail, I don't think. If you really take what you learn and you implement it and you follow and you ask questions along the way, I don't see how you can fail. And stay true to yourself, that's probably the other piece of it.

Mike Koenigs: All right. Well, let's give Karol a giant hand, Karol Clark! Wow, nice job! That was beautiful!

Karol Clark: Thank you!

Interview #4: Andy Falco - From Being a K9 Cop in Foreclosure and Bankruptcy to a $349,000 Deal in Less Than a Year

Mike Koenigs: Hi folks, here's Andy Falco. Pleasure to be speaking with you, Andy. So, if you recall when you came to our live event and took the hot seat where we gave you live coaching in front of several hundred people, can you tell what happened in the hot seat and where you are now? Can you share your story with us?

Andy Falco: I was broken and in debt. My house was nearing foreclosure. I had a need and a desire to figure my way out and I just had to do it. One of your staff, Robin, made it possible for me to attend an event that attended. I got in the hot seat with you and told my story of where I was and where I was hoping that I could go. I talked about my police dog training; my pet dog training; shared a book that I had… and you guys were brutally honest at my lowest moment, which was exactly what I needed. I took your advice, and at first, did only part of what you told me to do and had some success. I learned my lesson and then followed all of the things you guys told me to do. I was able to get my house out of foreclosure. I began to pay off all my bills, I became debt-free and then I just recently landed a contract with the country of Bahrain for $350,000.

Mike Koenigs: So I don't know about you, but that made me cry. That's what I live for. Thank you for that. That was a gift.

Male Speaker: That's what you live for.

Mike Koenigs: Yes, sir. Thank you. Congratulations! You made my life.

Now, I'll tell you what, you do that three times; you've got stories, you've got books, you've got TV and just about any of that stuff you can think of. But when that's what happens and you're not doing it for that reason, people can see what you're all about. If their hearts are open, their minds will follow. You cannot fake it; or if you can, you can't fake it for long. So just tap into that and pay attention in interviews and talk to your customers and find out what's going on. So, a huge part of why we're doing what we're doing here right now is to find you and to observe and experience that sparkle. It's that breakthrough; it's that moment. For you, it took two years to hit; but I we can't forget the incremental progress, and there's a lot more behind the story than what he just told you.

But that set-up, the only thing you left out on or you missed out on… I'm going to ask you this question, which is really a continuation; tell us how many kids you have and what it's like with your wife now.

Andy Falco: So you're trying to get me to cry? I left that out on purpose.

Mike Koenigs: What the courageous start, everyone will follow you every single time; so be raw. Just tell us.

Andy Falco: I was a police officer for 24 years and strong-willed, very manly and I thought I had everything. I had houses, I had cars and we were doing really well. When I lost everything, it took everything out of me. To share on the stage what I was going through was not that easy. I just knew that I'd hit the bottom.

I've got five children. Some of them are very young, even though I look like I wouldn't have young children, but I love them dearly and to think… I also forgot to say that I had to sleep in my car at the event because I couldn't afford a hotel room and had to borrow money for gas to get there from Orange County, California down to San Diego. If I'm sleeping in my car now, I'm going to have to find a way to sleep in the car with my family. They relied on me and I felt that I let them down; so there was just no other option. I wouldn't accept failure and I had realized that Mike and his team were where I was going to hang my hat. It happened to be the same event that you shared that you had been diagnosed with cancer and that was, although not on purpose, a very important thing for me to hear.

Everything you had to say at that point, as I shared the other day on a live event, I had with you guys, that you guys had become family. I love you guys dearly and I'll do anything for any of you. Everything that you have said to follow, when I follow it, it works. I have written a book and didn't follow; it didn't go to #1. I wrote another book, I followed and it went to #1. Everything that I have currently, I owe to God and I owe you guys and I appreciate it.

Mike Koenigs: Share what your wife says now and what your children say now?

Andy Falco: We nearly divorced a couple of times. It was bad. Of course, I get defensive. I don't need to be reminded of the things that I had failed to do, but I guess I did and so it wasn't good and we were on the verge of getting divorced. We are a blessed family. We are so happy. She has noticed the transformation. She has told people at our church how things are different now. It is a pleasure to be married again. It is a pleasure to be a father because now I feel like they have somebody to look up to. I didn't feel that they had somebody to look up to before. They don't know the whole story, but it is amazing what they see in you because they're watching you all the time in how you walk, in how you talk and I ask more questions about myself; seemingly now more from my experience with my children than I was before. I think it's because of that presence and the way that I present myself now and talk and share with others.

I've been asked to speak now at men's groups on topics of failure and success, about being fearlessly successful; and "fearlessly" is the important part, because I was so afraid that I was not going to be able to do what you guys had taught. I was not going to be able to write that book because I was so afraid that I didn't have the intelligence. Then again, my "self-permission" was one thing that Ed taught me: that I am an expert in a few areas, dog training would be one of them and now marketing. To be able to give myself permission to be an expert has changed my family, my business and my private life. So that's a great transformation.

Mike Koenigs: So tell me about your future. What do you see in your future? What's going to happen next?

Andy Falco: Clearly, my future is helping others and teaching them. That's a blanket statement that I'm sure everybody wants to do, but I have a story. I had a story before. I really have a story now. The police dog business has been instrumental in my life; the fact is that my dog literally saved my life. There was a guy that was going to kill me who was hiding behind the door with a gun and without my dog, I would not be here today. So my story in the dog training business is a tribute to him, and what I want to do as far as changing how police dogs are trained and teach humane forms of training and then using that platform, it will lead me into helping others with their business and finding their story, finding their avatar and then creating a business and a way to give it away to help the younger men in our society who need help. Being 20 right now is not easy with the distractions of the internet and with TV; and the perception of men in our world today needs to change, I think.

Mike Koenigs: Awesome!

Andy Falco: Thank you very much.

Female: We'd also like to you thank you and your team.

Mike Koenigs: I'm just a vessel, that's all. So thank you for that. Thank you. That's a gift. I've got my second chance in life after cancer. Every day is a gift.

Now, those things; the only way for them to happen is by getting in the game, and it's starting and doing it and embracing perfection and just being courageous and standing up and opening up your heart and having courage. I'll tell you, when you first walked on stage, I saw a broken man. Your body language and your physiology was that of a man not being able to provide for his family. I think it's one of the most difficult experiences a man can endure – feeling helpless. It's the sense of being an outcast in your own family, right?

At the same time, if you look at it from a story perspective, this is a resurrection story; it's the Christ story in motion. Our brains are hardwired to respond and react to this! Whether it is Jesus Christ or a mythical Christ figure, we cannot help but feel connected to it. It is what is in us. So going on that journey and taking our clients through that journey, we want drama; we cannot help it. It is what we are in the physical course of things from birth to death, right? So these questions are designed to evoke the transformational story, the resurrection story. Every time you can open up a chapter in your book of your own resurrection story, and it comes from service. Crucifixion is very, very symbolic; that's why Christianity is what it is to this day, right? It doesn't matter if you're a Christian or not, just pay attention to what's you're feeling. What does that symbolize and what does it mean?

So take your customers and your clients on that journey and they will love you, but it's got to come from a bare, raw, authentic place, so that we can celebrate in your own resurrection story. Look, it doesn't have to be like his. This isn't about creating and making something up, it's just being real, all right? We all have it going on. Something is going on inside us right now, I guarantee it. It's the human experience. It's the only way to break through the next level.

Interview #5: Carlos Carrera - The "Tony Robbins of Mexico"

Mike Koenigs: From Mexico, we have Carlos Carrera. Our Latinos and Latinas who are here with us today are very proud of Carlos. What's great about Carlos is, he is a rapid implementer. He's been taking our tools and resources to a different country. A lot of people ask us, "Will this work in my business? Will this work in my country? Will this work in my language?" The answer is an absolute yes. Carlos has been using all the tools and all the resources in really transforming lives; so you can understand why I call Carlos the "Tony Robbins of Mexico."

Carlos Carrera: Thank you! Gracias!

Mike Koenigs: Yes. So let's go through and tell your story here step-by-step. So we have a picture of your first book right here and it's *Reclama Tu Poder Personal...* and I know I butchered that but I did the best that I could.

Carlos Carrera: Yes.

Mike Koenigs: *Reclaim Your Personal Power.*

Carlos Carrera: You got it.

Mike Koenigs: So what has happened as a result of your book? Why don't you tell us?

Carlos Carrera: Well because of my book, first of all, it gave me so much focus about my mission in life. So now, I don't have to take carrots from different people. People come to me and they make me offers, they say, "Well, I want you to be a manager of these salespeople," and then I will say, "Thank you! Thank you! Thank you!" So my book, because of my book, now I can serve, help and really share the best of myself with people and they can have authentic real transformation.

Mike Koenigs: That's very nice. Okay, here's another one. I put the fire on there because one of your team members is giving a pose that only a beautiful Latina can make, it seems. She's "El Fuego," is that right?" It's not "La Fuego, it's "El Fuego," see? [A Latina woman in the audience shared some very "Latina-like" movements at the moment.]

Carlos Carrera: Yes.

Mike Koenigs: Okay, but tell me about this. What's this? [shows photos of crowds of people he has helped]

Carlos Carrera: Well because of the book, people, they see you like a celebrity; honestly, because assume they are going to come for the conference and they know that you have a book, they go like, "Oh, give me an autograph. Oh my God!" And you can feel how nervous people are in front of you because they shake your hand and their hand is sweating.

Mike Koenigs: Shaking and trembling, yeah.

Carlos Carrera: Yes, like, "Oh my God!" So it's much, much, much easier to make friends; and other people, they want to come and help you in your mission. Oh my God! So much easier. So you can choose which people are good for your mission, so you don't have to have problems with people.

Mike Koenigs: So your team are people who are genuine believers in your mission and the vision and in what you're doing? We call this indoctrination – they read and listen to your books, listen to your podcasts, watch your videos, buy your products, attend your events, join your masterminds. They're customers first!

Carlos Carrera: Yes.

Mike Koenigs: That's very powerful. All right, and then this - I know one of the things that you do is you're an avid user of all of our tools and resources. You and all of your clients and customers are using them. But you just showed me something earlier; your 14-year-old son is also using the tools and he's building his own platform.

Carlos Carrera: We were talking about this because my son came to my training by the name of "Maximal Commitment"; and in only three weeks, he changed his mentality. He just turned 14 years old. At the time, I said to him, "Would you love to write a book? This is what a book has been doing for me. Would you like to have the same thing?" He looked at me like, "Me, dad?" I said, "Yes, of course. If you are willing to get into a maximal commitment, we'll do it together." And I got the cover and I took the pictures for him and I started to develop everything and I taught him how to create his own website; and in exactly two days, we have everything. Then I asked him, "You know, you have to write 10 questions about what people are going to ask you and questions that people don't know about it, but you do; but they have to come from your heart, from what you believe."

So he started to type. The next day we were in the gym and this lady from another state of Mexico shows up and he starts to talk to her and then I said to her, "This is my son. He is the author of *Adolescente Imparable*." When I started to talk like that, she was like, "How old are you?" My son is "14." "Oh my God! You already have a book. How come?" Then we took the telephone and we showed her that this is my son and he has his book, and from that moment it's been like my son has changed his self-image. Now every time, everywhere he goes he says, "I'm the author of *Adolescente Imparable*, and people treat him like a very intelligent person. So his entire self-image changed completely. Now, he doesn't want to eat meat; he wants to exercise everyday; he wants to be congruent with his book. For me as a father, it is the best gift that life can ever give me; the best of the best of the best.

Mike Koenigs: Yeah, and I think that's the sign of a great dad too, right? So that's a great "because of my book" story. Congratulations! That's a tearjerker. It's given you a gift as well. Moving on... who are these people here?

Carlos Carrera: Well, many of these people I used to watch on TV; and because of my book, now I have access to celebrities. I have pictures of me with them and we're working together!

I never thought I was going to be able to meet them; to shake their hands. Some of them, they stay in my house; some of them, they have sold like more than a million copies of their records and all that. It's amazing.

Mike Koenigs: Yeah. Who are these people for folks who don't know? Like top left to...

Carlos Carrera: Well, the lady on the right side, my right side, she's on TV every morning. She's very famous because of the gossip show she does. The one in the bottom, on the right side, she's Tere Bermea. She's been on TV and radio and she talks about self-improvement, spirituality and all that. The other lady - oh my God! She's in movies, she's like, super gorgeous, she's tall and - I mean, that picture of her is one of my favorite pictures.

This is called, "celebrity attachment." That gives you so much power to negotiate. Then sometimes people, they see me on Facebook and they see me with all these movie stars and it's like an automatic trust and relationship.

Mike Koenigs: Yeah. Very nice!

Carlos Carrera: Because there are people who want to be with other people that are with celebrities, with people that are making a difference.

Mike Koenigs: Yeah. Beautiful, beautiful! Who's this?

Carlos Carrera: Oh my God! This is super incredible. His name is Fernando Allende. He's been in movies with the most beautiful actresses in Mexico and Latin America, but also he made movies in Hollywood. A company hired me to give training and then he was singing mariachi and I was like, "Oh my God! I know this guy." I said, "Wow! It's Fernando Allende." And then I said to myself, "You know what? He's nice. He must be like over 65 years old and he's in great shape. Probably he's staying in the same hotel. So if I see him I'm going to ask him for an autograph."

So the next day, I'm having breakfast right there in the hotel and he's at the front desk and I said to myself, "This is my opportunity." So I go to run into him; but before I can, he is walking towards me and then he looked at me and he said, "Carlos Carrera?" He opens his briefcase, he takes my book out and then said, "Please, would you give me an autograph and would you sell me another book for my son in Puerto Rico?" I'm like… I would never forget this because I was signing his book and then everything started to spin around me and I was thinking, "Oh my God! He is the famous person! Why is he asking me for an autograph?"

I in a different dimension. He didn't have any idea what he did for me. Fernando Allende changed the life, the history of Mexico; because later on I was thinking, "Oh my God! Your book makes you beautiful, attractive, it makes you a celebrity; it makes you interesting." So even if you don't have a career, your book gives you all this perspective. Because of him, I said, "You know what? Now, I'm going to train people to write their own books. Now I'm going to train people to create their own books and change everything," because thanks to Fernando Allende, the Transformational Academy started.

Mike Koenigs: Oh, this is beautiful! All right, and who is this?

Carlos Carrera: Oh my God! This guy is so famous. Everybody that is over 35 years old knows this guy. His name is Franco, he sings a famous song 'Toda La Vida' and -

Mike Koenigs: Sing it.

Female Speaker: "Toda la vida."

Carlos Carrera: "Toda la vida." Yeah, he's very famous and because of my book, he went to my house, he wanted to know the author of the *Reclaim Your Personal Power* and basically he came and did a training with me. I helped him because he had what I call "celebrity syndrome," something that Marilyn Monroe, Elvis Presley, Whitney Houston; people that were very successful with a lot of fame but didn't have significance. That's why they start doing drugs and all that because once you master something, you have to help other people; you have to serve; you have to give; you have to share and help other people master what you've already mastered; otherwise, you get stuck; you don't really become happy and grateful.

So this guy had the same challenge and he understood that he needed to share what he did in the Latino market with musicians, and we created this book by the name of *Toda La Vida Maximo Compromiso*, on how a person can position themselves in first place in their niche; in their field. Really, really fascinating; because this guy did it and he had this song for more than 30 weeks in the States, Mexico, South America… and he basically became a very powerful friend. And because of Franco, I started to have my trainings with a very powerful celebrity that sings at my trainings and all that. So because of my book, I've been able to have these beautiful connections.

Because of my book, also, it opened the doors for me to TV, to radio. This lady on the left side, her name is Janet Arceo. She has the most powerful reputation. She's a beautiful angel. She's been on TV and radio, and I meet with her all the time and she said, "You know, Carlos. I don't like when people give courses and they're not congruent, but I read your book and I see what you do with people." You remember that we brought lots of people from my tribe who used your system to write their books?

Mike Koenigs: Your team to our event?

Carlos Carrera: Yeah.

Mike Koenigs: Yeah, that was great. I know you just told me before we started that you're bringing another group and another team.

Carlos Carrera: Yes. I'm bringing more people to your next event because now they know about Mike, they know about your entire team. So they're very excited to come because they know that you are the only person to come to. I have been taking trainings since I was 21 years old with Tony Robbins, Brian Tracy, Zig Ziglar, Mark Victor Hanson, Jack Canfield, Jim Rohn, Wayne Dyer, Deepak Chopra… but I have never seen anybody that has a team like you; it's unbelievable, and I'm modeling myself based on you in Mexico.

I used to say that you said that I'm the "Tony Robbins" of Mexico. Now, I'm telling people I'm the "Mike Koenigs" of Mexico. But really, you are a true example, because I've been with you the last three years and I've been taking everything. I have all of your programs, all of them. I love everything that you do; everything that you offer; but the most important thing is how you've been able to work as a team and maintain your team. That is like "Mission Impossible" for most people.

Carlos Carrera: Well, because of my book, I get awards now all the time. They give me these awards because a lot of people that are getting results because of my book; because my book is about self-sabotage; how you can reprogram yourself even faster; about love and how the emotions can make you accomplish all these goals; but at the same time how you can sabotage yourself and you can end up with a terrible disease.

Because of that, a lot of people, they've been getting a lot of powerful results; and because of my book, I'm getting recognitions; awards I never thought that were possible. Suddenly, I get a letter; they go like, "Well, the Association of Women, they want to give you this award." I'm like, "Wow!" And then with the awards it comes also the business; it's great how you can have balance between your spirituality and money.

So you can honestly help people by having your maximum freedom and then you can go and train people to achieve the same goals.

Mike Koenigs: Beautiful! And this?

Carlos Carrera: Well, the trainings keep growing, baby. I mean, this is really good because I always tell people, "Information is power," and people go like, "Yes"; and then I always tell them, "No!" That's a big lie. Information without action is no power. So when you get information, the first thing that you have to do is you must decide and take massive action. If you take massive action, you get massive results. If you take little action, you get little results. If you take no action, there are no results. So as Stephen Covey used to say, "Knowing without doing is not power, it doesn't help you."

So in my trainings, because of my book, I've been able to give to people a step-by-step guide on what they have to do; and then my book, it transformed into different products.

Mike Koenigs: Let's keep on going here. So, are these kids or are they adults or are they both?

Carlos Carrera: Yeah, they're adults. I started to train people over 18, but then some people, they were like 16, but they look like 18 and 19. They got into my trainings with amazing results and I said, "Okay, I'm going to let people that are 16 come to my trainings," and then people - kids that were like 14 but looked like 16 or 17 - just started to come to my trainings like that.

So now, I take anybody; including kids that are 19 years old with a really mature mentality who say, "You know what? I saw how you transformed my mom, my dad. I want the same results. I want to have a lot of energy. I don't want to eat meat. I want to really have an amazing life." Now, I'm training a lot of people; and not just Mexico, also people from Central America and South America, they are coming now to my trainings in Mexico City.

Mike Koenigs: Beautiful, beautiful. All right, look at that. Okay. I know we've got some books here and there's actually something else that is very exciting, which you just told me about literally right before we started.

We'll get to that at the end, but you've got books, multiple books; so six of them, brand new and coming up.

Carlos Carrera: Yeah. What happens is that if you get massive results with one book, what do you do? You get another one and you get another one; but many of these, the rest of the books, I wrote these books as a team. So *El Despertar de tu Poder Tridimensional* and *Toda la Vida*, I wrote these books with other people because I believe in teamwork. It's faster; it's more powerful; you promote other people, they promote you; and then that's how you create your partners.

Mike Koenigs: Very nice.

Carlos Carrera: They support you and you support them.

Mike Koenigs: Beautiful. All right. And then what was this?

Carlos Carrera: Wow! I get tired of people telling me that I am crazy - because I always tell people that your first mission in life is to find, to discover your mission in life.

Mike Koenigs: That's one of the troubles of being an action-taker; sometimes you're also a maverick, a cowboy and a pioneer so you've got arrows in your back!

Carlos Carrera: Yes. So I said, "You know what? From Jesus Christ, Buddha, Mother Theresa, Gandhi, Osho; all of them, they talk about two things: the awakening and your mission. Most trainings, they just talk about that, but they don't really make you go inside of you to synchronize the purpose of your mind, the passion of your heart and the significance of your spirit. So, I went outside, I got these people that helped me to write this book, *El Despertar de tu Poder Tridimensional*, which means *The Awakening of Your Three-Dimensional Power*, and I said, "We are going to make a movie."

So we went to interview people everywhere in Mexico with a really high level of consciousness and a really low level of consciousness and we're going to ask them three questions, "What's a job for you, what's a vocation, and what's a mission?" It doesn't matter who you ask this question. Everybody agreed that better than a job is your vocation; and much, much better than your vocation is your mission. Then I ask to people, "What about if you can make a lot of money with your mission in life?" And people, every single one, they were like, "Well, that will be the perfect life." So how come they're not doing it?

So this movie shows that at the root of so many millions of people, they have this life of quiet desperation; they have this life in which they don't use their full personal power because they haven't discovered their mission. It's like riding a horse. You can be riding the horse in the same direction that the horse is going, but most people, they're going backwards. So they make their life more difficult. So this movie basically shows the power of discovering your mission in life.

Mike Koenigs: Right. So you've got an opportunity to make a movie because of your book, too?

Carlos Carrera: Yes.

Mike Koenigs: Obviously, you've been very successful with this and here are some of your programs. We're going to go through some of these but tell us very quickly about that.

Carlos Carrera: Well, once you have your book, you can start your escalation - which is something I learned from you and Pam Hendrickson; very powerful with your system because the book, you can transform your book into a conference; a seminar; a training; a coaching program; a certification.

You can record your own audios, make your own videos. I mean, now, I love these platforms with memberships where you can put all your videos, audios, PDFs; and then you don't have to carry all this stuff and then you can travel, sell all your products. People, they love it because once they take your training, they can get onto their telephone and they can continue watching videos and all of that. So because of my book, that book is like a transformer. It transforms into different materials; and with this, you can really help people to achieve their goals.

Mike Koenigs: Beautiful, beautiful. And here's another one, what does this represent?

Carlos Carrera: Once you have a book, once you start to create momentum and you start to create products and take trainings, they have celebrity attachments and then you get a powerful platform. So when I'm travelling, I get in an airplane or if I'm in a restaurant, I always go like, "Hey! Nice meeting you. What's your name? What do you do?" When you ask the people about their names and what do they do, later on they're going to ask you what's your name and what do you do. Then I say, "Well, I'm an author of a book in Amazon by the name of *Reclaim Your Personal Power* and I have this passion to help people to achieve maximum freedom and make more money," and all that. And I say, "Well, this is me." And they go like, "Oh my God!" Suddenly, their face changes. Suddenly, there's an instant connection. There's a relationship, trust. In my trainings, I always ask people, "Tell me the first thing that comes to your mind when you know that someone has a book." They go, "Well, they're organized. They know what they want. They are experts. They are like, different." Every single person always has something powerful to say about someone that has a book.

Now, what I tell to people, "Now, tell me about salesmen. What do you think about a salesman?" "They are going to pressurize me. They're going to lie to me. They are going to take my money," and all that. And I say, "See? Your book is your best business card. Your book is your best flyer. It's like a magic key that will open doors to you, that right now they're closed. Doors that are so high, but now you can fly and you can open and achieve."

Mike Koenigs: Beautiful, beautiful. So before I ask you about this - and maybe I will ask you - what does this represent here?

Carlos Carrera: So in the beginning, people took my basic training, "Maximum Commitment," which I used to help people to discover their mission in life with an unspecified name. But then later on, a lot of people wouldn't do too much. Why? Because people will say, "Well, you are crazy. You are what? What is that?" So people, they are expecting that you say, "Well, I'm a doctor." "I'm a lawyer." "I'm an accountant," and all that. Well, your secret mission has to have a specific name that no-one of the more than 160,000 million people that have been on this earth, they never ever had.

So your book gives you a path. Your book is your star. Your book is your GPS. Your book, you know, makes you work toward your track. That's how I created the Transformation Academy. So I started to take people into my house. I started to share all the secrets and I started to create this hybrid model

Carlos Carrera: A hybrid of selling and negotiation and marketing and technology. So now in seven weeks, I can teach people how to sell, negotiate, how to write the books, how to use your systems... and then how they can have a powerful platform. So when they talk to people, they go like, "This is me." When they show the book, they're going to be like, "Oh wow!" So people that are closing business faster, they get a lot of recognition. So now, they're starting to get the same results that I'm getting.

Mike Koenigs: To talk a little bit about how our certification programs have helped build and helped you create your academy and the tools and training, because you showed me this earlier and your academy grows every time. That first picture was this first group and then the second and the third and it's just building up and up and up; but how has the certification helped you?

Carlos Carrera: Well, let me give you an idea. Let me show you an example. When I come to the certifications, you give us so much detail, but also you pushed us in a way that we take action. For example, you told us about recording our book. You told us that it has to be 10 minutes. Then when I walked next to you, you go like, "You better do that," like you were expecting the best of me; and guess what?

Mike Koenigs: So holding you to a higher standard?

Carlos Carrera: A higher standard.

Mike Koenigs: All right.

Carlos Carrera: And guess what? I did it.

Mike Koenigs: That's great. One of the things that I know you did (and we've got two transformational mini stories here), you've basically taken our certification model, brought it to Mexico and are implementing it and have basically done what we've been teaching, which is to do it with your book service.

Carlos Carrera: Yes.

Mike Koenigs: Which we've been providing and teaching people how to do. So here, you've got a transformational story. So can you just tell the story about what happened with this woman here?

Carlos Carrera: Sure. So, America Maldonado, she knows a lot about her stuff, but she didn't have a platform.

Mike Koenigs: Yeah.

Carlos Carrera: So soon, she started to create her platform; she started to really take massive action and that's because she changed her self-image about how she sees herself. So you can see that before and after, it's amazing how people really transform and now how they start to walk and talk their mission in life.

Mike Koenigs: Very nice, very nice. And then again, this is something you shared. These are screen captures of all of your clients and students that you've helped using these tools to write books; become bestselling authors; build their platform. Now, you're podcasting as well. So every single time we come up with something new, you implement it and you bring it to your clients and your customers. It's very, very impressive.

This image here, tell me a little bit about this and what's happening for you in your speaking career and also when you go out, now that you've got all these different packages that you've created.

Carlos Carrera: Because of my book, basically, what I did was I increased my closing percentage. In the past, when I used to talk in front of people, my closing percentage was about 30%, 40%.

But because of my book, I can recommend to take action and then I always tell people, "You know what? Now, there are a lot of people coming to take my training and they have signed up for several different courses. So I tell them, "You can take my training anytime you want, and this is how much will be the investment," and then I separate every single thing. Then I say, "But if you take "Massive Action" now, I'm going to give you a discount. I'm going to give you this bonus, this bonus, this bonus. I'm going to give you this incentive. I'm going to give you financing and I'm going to make it so easy that you would be crazy not to do it." Because of my book, I can recommend people to take massive action. Why? Because people, they know what I'm talking about.

So my book has been giving me testimonials, has been giving me pictures of celebrity attachment. It has been given me so many tools that people, when they come to me, they go like, "Wow! I've never seen anything like this before." My closing percentage with my audience is from 80% to a 100%.

Female Speaker: Wow!

Mike Koenigs: That's beautiful, beautiful. Here's the last thing. So you've been here; you're going through the new training; next, there's the certification training; and one of our assignments that we gave in this new course is to go back and record your new book. We created a cover, went through a new process. Again (right before we started the video, this is what was taking me a little while to get prepared), you showed me something on your phone. Why don't you tell me what you did?

Carlos Carrera: You and your team always inspire me, and I know that I have to take massive action because that's part of my philosophy and basically I said, "You know what? I'm going to do it."

I started my book yesterday, and I started to record it and I made sure that I had every single question and continued recording. Even this morning, I still needed to finish some chapters, and I was in the shower, so I put my telephone on outside and I continue talking and talking and I have the blow drier also, you will hear that with the blow drier. Then, I was driving here in the studio and I was recording the last part because I knew that I would say, "Well, how much time do I need? Ten minutes for every chapter?" So I planned exactly when I had to start it and when I was going to finish and guess what? I show it to you.

Mike Koenigs: Yes.

Carlos Carrera: I finished my book today. The most important thing is for me to take massive action.

Mike Koenigs: So tell everyone what you did in under 24 hours - because this is the book cover of your brand new book that's coming out - and what did you do? [I show a picture of Carlo's new book cover on screen that was designed over night]

How much of your book did you finish?

Carlos Carrera: Everything. Done.

Mike Koenigs: Okay. So, how do you like that? Carlos walked up to me this morning and he said, "I did my whole book last night and this morning, it's done. I finished 20 chapters, 10 minutes each," he followed the system step-by-step. So I think he won the prize, congratulations! The bottom line is, Carlos, you're a massive action-taker and we love that you're in the program and part of the certification program; and I love the fact that you're bringing this internationally as well because more people deserve to experience what their book will give them. Again, going back to that beautiful phrase, "because of my book"; you're a living shining example of what's possible.

So let's give Carlos a giant hand. Congratulations! Very beautiful.

Carlos Carrera: Viva Mexico!

Mike Koenigs: Viva Mexico! Si!

So one question, just raise your hand if you recorded a significant part of your book since you've been here. You finished? No, not finished. Okay. A significant part finished? Okay. Check it out! All right, that's very impressive. So our goal is to increase that. Congratulations! [We have a group of people raise their hands in the training who started recording their book in just one day]

So what do you think of this man? Is he awesome? Great job. To me, the big bonus was what you've done with your son. That's really beautiful man. Thank you for being here!

Carlos Carrera: No, thank you; because there was a time when I was really lost with technology, with systems; I was frustrated because I was given little training, but I knew I had to get into technology, I knew I had to be able to offer to people something that they could grab; something they could watch and all that. I started to check everybody and I found you; and then so since I found you I said, "Wow! This man has everything in one place." So now, all my life, it's in this telephone. You what I'm going to do next year? This is like a goal. I want to go to Central America and South America, just with a t-shirt, jeans, no money; just my passport and my telephone. The goal is that in less than 30 days, in 30 days, I have to be living in a really nice house, I have to have a car, I have to be helping a lot of people, I have to make a lot of friends, but most importantly, create an impact in 30 days. So I'm going to be recording; I want to put my video on the podcast so people can see this. I'm going to show to people that they can make more than $10,000 or more than a 100,000 pesos in 30 days if you have the right platform.

OTHER BOOKS BY MIKE KOENIGS

Make Market Launch IT: The Ultimate Product Creation System for Turning Your Ideas Into Income

Top Gun Consulting: How to Create a Fun and Lucrative Business Sharing Your Knowledge, Experience or Story

You Everywhere Now: Get Your Message, Products and Services in Front of Your Target Prospects and in Every Pocket, Screen, Car and Television in the World with the Help of the Largest Brands

Publish and Profit: A 5-Step System for Attracting Paying Coaching and Consulting Clients, Traffic and Leads, Product Sales and Speaking Engagements

How to Be a Video Interview Pro: 25 Strategies to Get ATTENTION and Make Your YouTube, Livestream, Google Hangouts, Skype Interviews and Videos Look or Sound Like a Professional TV or Radio Show

OTHER PROGRAMS AND PRODUCTS BY MIKE KOENIGS

Quickly start your own online interactive TV show or infomercial channel to build an audience, list and promote your products, services or brand...even if you aren't a techie. This is the ultimate video marketing training system for entrepreneurs, small business owners, authors, experts, speakers, coaches, consultants and creative types.

What is the "Webcast Profit Toolkit"?

Have you ever watched an infomercial on TV or online and wondered how they're made and whether or not one could be made about your products, services or you and sell your products in a highly interactive and educational way to make money for you without having to sell in person, on stage and at little or no expense?

What if it was easy to do and took just a couple of hours to get started with equipment you already own and know how to use?

The Webcast Profit Toolkit is a live and online training course that teaches entrepreneurs, small business owners, authors, experts, speakers, coaches, consultants and creative types how to start their own *Interactive Online Television Shows* to sell or create products and services.

"Webcasts" are just like TV infomercials except they are interactive and can be produced and broadcast for free using equipment you already own and know how to use. The Webcast Profit Toolkit teaches you how to use low-cost computers and camera equipment and produce a compelling, educational, entertaining business show that gets viewers interested in any product or service.

Visit **www.WebcastToolkit.com** for a free training webcast and more information.

BOOK MIKE TO SPEAK!

Book Mike Koenigs as your Keynote Speaker and You're Guaranteed to Make Your Event Highly Entertaining and Unforgettable!

For over two decades, Mike Koenigs has been educating, entertaining and helping entrepreneurs, authors, experts, speakers, consultants and coaches build and grow their businesses with the online video, social media, mobile and product creation strategies.

His origin story includes his recent near-death brush with stage 3a cancer, growing up lower middle-class in a small town in Eagle Lake Minnesota, severe ADHD and "meeting" Tony Robbins through an infomercial that changed his life forever. After successfully building and exiting from two companies and selling them to publicly-traded companies, Mike can share relevant, actionable strategies that anyone can use - even if they're starting from scratch.

His unique style inspires, empowers and entertains audiences while giving them the tools and strategies they need and want to get seen, heard, build and grow successful sustainable brands and businesses.

For more info, visit www.MikeKoenigs.com/speaking or call +1 (858) 412-0858.

Made in the USA
San Bernardino, CA
23 April 2016